THE WEST COUNTRY

Kynance Cove, Cornwall.

*Overleaf: view east-north-east from Sharpers
Head, across Gorah Rocks, South Devon.*

GREAT WALKS

THE WEST COUNTRY

JOHN WEIR

Photography by Stephen J. Whitehorne

WARD LOCK

First published in Great Britain in 1993
by Ward Lock Limited, Villiers House, 41/47 Strand,
London WC2N 5JE, England
A Cassell Imprint

Text filmset by August Filmsetting, Haydock, St Helens

Printed and bound in Slovenia
by printing house
DELO Tiskarna by arrangement with Korotan Italiana

CIP data for this book is available upon
application from The British Library.

ISBN 0 7063 6943 2

ACKNOWLEDGEMENTS

I must acknowledge the considerable help given to me by many people during the preparation of *Great Walks: the West Country*. In particular, I thank the publishers who had the vision to support such a book; Stephen Whitehorne, photographer, who gave encouragement, captured the beauty and interest of the walks selected, and who has managed to mirror the essence of place; Dartmoor and Exmoor National Park Authorities; the Quantock Hills Warden Service; the various County Planning Departments and District Councils who administer a wide range of countryside management schemes in the region, and those other bodies — statutory and voluntary — and individuals who, through their work, make great walks in the West Country possible; all those persons, many anonymous, who on the way gave me advice and local insight; Devon Library Services and the West Country Studies Library (Exeter), and all chroniclers, researchers and observers of West Country life past and present who have provided much inspiration.

Thank you also to Joyce Reardon for typing the manuscript; and to Margaret, Darren and Rachel for continual support and understanding.

John Weir

Contents

APPENDICES

INTRODUCTION

For the purpose of this book the West Country is defined as that part of England to the west of a line drawn from Portishead near Bristol to Poole Harbour in Dorset. It takes in the whole of Cornwall, Devon, Somerset, most of Dorset and a sliver of Avon, and from any point the coast is never far away — this 160 mile (257 km) long crooked finger has 600 miles (965 km) of coastline. Twenty-six miles (42 km) beyond Land's End are the Isles of Scilly.

The beginnings of any landscape are in its rocks and the earth processes that act upon them, and geologically and geomorphologically the South-West is a region of great contrasts. Its backbone consists of a major granite feature that emerges as a series of masses, including Dartmoor, Bodmin Moor, St Austell, Carnmenellis, Carn Brea, Penwith/Land's End and the Isles of Scilly. Exmoor is not granite, but its gritty Devonian sandstones also create high moors. A high limestone ridge, riddled with caves and cut with gorges, forms the Mendip Hills.

The south-west pensinula has the mildest climate in Britain. Its coastline is warmed by the Gulf Stream, and the prevailing south-westerlies bring moisture-laden air over the whole region. Most rain falls in the west of the region and on the higher land — highest Dartmoor can receive 100 in (2540 mm) a year. Mists and fogs are common. In parts of Dorset the rainfall drops to 30 in (762 mm). Across the whole region there are many winters without snow, and frosts are rare on the south Cornwall and south Devon coastlines. Here, south-facing sides of sheltered, narrow valleys can support a rich assemblage of plants introduced from sub-tropical climes.

Although once isolated by terrain and distance, human occupation has spanned many millenia; this combination has left its mark and continues to do so. Evidence abounds of past settlement and industrial activity such as peat-cutting, mining and quarrying. Farming dominates the scene, fishing much less so; more modern incursions — including forestry, reservoirs, larger-scale quarrying, agricultural improvement, military training, housing and industrial estates and tourist development — bring the landscape palimpsest up to date.

All areas are unique, but two facets set the West Country apart — the quality of light and the uniqueness of the region's landscape diversity when considered alongside other, comparatively-sized, areas of Britain. This diversity of landscape,

Moorland — a dominant component of the landscape of both Dartmoor and Exmoor.

embracing nature and culture, is mirrored by the diversity and extent of designation for conservation and protection and, where applicable, livelihood and recreation — two National Parks, some 370 miles (594 km) of Heritage Coasts, 1188 sq miles (3084 sq km) of Areas of Outstanding Natural Beauty, numerous Sites of Special Scientific Interest, internationally important National Nature Reserves, several Environmentally Sensitive Areas, and Britain's longest National Trail. And beyond the boundaries of such designations, efforts are made by many land-owners and others to ensure that protected areas do not become islands in a sea of second-class environments.

Inevitably, the West Country is one of Britain's favourite holiday destinations. Tourism is necessary, green tourism is critical — for Cornwall, the tourist industry has overtaken agri-culture in economic importance. However, when the need arises, it is easy to escape the full beaches, the clotted cream and pasties, the caravans and chalets. There are many unfrequented places, and that crowded beach on a Bank Holiday can be a 'wilderness' at dawn or in the dead of winter.

Public access in the region has been much improved in recent years. Within Exmoor and Dartmoor National Parks over 1200 miles (1931 km) of paths — public rights-of-way and permitted paths — exist. Exmoor, Bodmin Moor, Dartmoor, the Quan-tocks and the West Penwith Moors have extensive tracks of moorland which extend walking possibilities. The two National Park Authorities, and local authorities responsible for Heritage Coasts, the South-West Coast Path National Trail and other areas, have undertaken comprehensive waymarking of the path network: maintenance and improvements are on-going tasks. The information given within the route descriptions in this book, as far as is known, was accurate when collected. However, legal diversions and possible future access agreements may result in deviations — always use up-to-date maps when possible.

With an Ordnance Survey Landranger, Pathfinder or Outdoor Leisure Map in hand, it is virtually impossible for the walker not to encounter something of interest with most miles walked. In this sense, and given the extensive walking opportunities that exist, the selection of walks has been a difficult task. The walks chosen, however, do give a good geographical spread for the South-West and will introduce the walker to most of the penin-sula's distinct areas — places where you can spend years of exploration and never weary of it. But this book does not include the recognized and/or established great walks of the South-West,

The ridge path on West Cliff and Cathole Cliff, between Bolt Tail and Bolt Head on the South Devon Heritage Coast.

9

Death Steps, Pednevounder Beach (National Trust) on the Penwith Heritage Coast.

such as the Two Moors Way, the Abbots' Way or the Mendip Way; they have been adequately dealt with elsewhere. A great walk is not so much determined by its length or historical origins, but more by the way it is trod. I hope the routes described here will lead to your own great walks, your own inner essays on the landscape.

The West Country is largely free from sources of industrial pollution and is characterized by a clarity of air and a vividness of colour. Its beauty lies in the land, the water, and in the air above. For many, the need to feel and experience a sense of place on one's own terms is a fundamental reality; the South-West peninsula enables you to fulfil that need.

J.W.H.W.

A PHOTOGRAPHER'S VIEW

A great mistake when discovering the countryside is to pass it by all too quickly. The West Country, with its many varied moods and landscapes, deserves a contemplative approach. Looking, lingering and hedge-poking were prerequisites for capturing on film more than just first impressions or chance images. In particular, the project became a search for that special quality of light on the land, a pursuit which makes landscape photography essentially a waiting game.

Rather less enjoyable, though equally necessary, was the need to cope with the logistics of all-weather and every-season photography. These practicalities proved a significant handicap to progress — the repetitive burden of photographic equipment carried across remote moors, over muddy levels and on often unstable coastal paths ensured that. But, I have come to love England's South-West peninsula, even when Dartmoor's unforgiving granite claimed one of my cherished OMIN bodies!

While aiming to achieve representative photographs, I also reserve some concern over displaying 'appealing' images. It seems that the biggest threat to our countryside comes not from the bulldozer or the plough but from our spiritual, emotional and physical detachment from it. The growing affection for images of the countryside, rather than for the countryside itself, is a worrying one. In the context of this book, I hope the photographs will help fuel an appetite for a discovery of the real West Country. They were never intended to be a substitute for it.

Finally I should like to say special thanks to John and Margaret Weir who, on my numerous trips out West, have generously accommodated me and guided me over unfamiliar ground.

S.J.W.

The Face of the West Country

The National Parks and Other Designated Areas

Dartmoor and Exmoor National Parks

In 1945 John Dower defined a National Park, as applied to Great Britain, as 'an extensive area of beautiful and relatively wild country in which, for the nation's benefit and by appropriate national decision and action, (a) the characteristic landscape beauty is strictly preserved, (b) access and facilities for public open-air enjoyment are amply provided, (c) wildlife and buildings and places of architectural and historic interest are suitably protected, while (d) established farming use is effectively maintained'.

Of the twelve National Parks in England and Wales, two — Dartmoor and Exmoor — are situated in the south-west part of England. Dartmoor National Park lies wholly within the county of Devon, between Exeter to the east and Plymouth to the west. Twenty-five miles (40 km) to the north-north-east, straddling Devon and Somerset and visible from Dartmoor, lies Exmoor National Park. Together they extend for some 630 sq miles (1631 sq km). Both areas have unique qualities which make them distinctively Dartmoor and Exmoor.

Dartmoor is the largest and wildest open space in southern England. The core of the National Park is an upland of granite rising to 2038 ft (621 m) at High Willhays — this is the highest land in England south of Kinder Scout (2088 ft, 636 m) in the Peak District, some 250 miles (402 km) away. Two vast blocks of moorland, in the north and south, are separated by the River Dart and its tributaries. Surrounding this moorland is Dartmoor's 'in-country' — an intimate enclosed landscape containing islands of common land. The moorland is characterized by wide expanses of bog and smooth contoured hills often crowned by rugged tors; here is the greatest density of prehistoric remains in north-western Europe. Mist and cloud frequently shroud the hills and the average rainfall is high. Streams and rivers rise in bogs and their valleys are wide in the upper reaches; where they leave the moor they cascade down waterfalls and run through rolling gorges in steep, wooded valleys.

Exmoor contains a wide variety of landscapes despite its comparatively small size. Unlike most other south-west moorlands, Exmoor does not consist of granite; Devonian sedimentary rocks dominate most of the geology. The central plateau comprises sweeping moorland, and to the north the land meets the sea abruptly in towering cliffs above the Bristol Channel. Here rocky headlands, steep, wooded ravines and waterfalls combine to make this an area of exceptional beauty. The Exmoor panorama is also enhanced by deep, wooded valleys and beech-hedged pasture. Dunkery Beacon, the highest point on Exmoor, rises to 1704 ft (520 m).

The Dartmoor and Exmoor National Park Authorities' responsibilities are geared to the twin purposes of National Parks — the conservation and enhancement of the quality of the landscape and the promotion of the enjoyment of that landscape by the public.

Much of the unique landscape of the Somerset Levels has been designated an Environmentally Sensitive Area.

HERITAGE COASTS

There are over 40 Heritage Coasts in England and Wales defined by the Countryside Commission, with a combined length of some 907 miles (1460 km). Of this total, about 369 miles (594 km) i.e. 40 per cent, lies in the West Country. All have a unique beauty and identity. Some lengths of coast are owned by the local authority, others are protected by English Nature or by voluntary bodies such as the National Trust. But, like our National Parks, much of the coast remains in the hands of private landowners and farmers. Overall and financial responsibility for Heritage Coasts normally lies with District or County Councils, and many have appointed Heritage Coast Officers. On the South-West peninsula, stretches of Heritage Coast include the Isles of Scilly (40 miles, 64 km), Pentire Point–Widemouth (33.5 miles, 54 km), Trevose Head, St Agnes, Penwith (34 miles, 55 km), the Lizard (17 miles, 28 km), the Roseland (33.5 miles, 54 km), Gribbin Head–Polperro, and Rame Head – all in Cornwall; in Devon are the East Devon (17 miles, 25 km) and South Devon (46 miles, 74 km) Heritage Coasts, and Lundy Island; straddling Devon and Cornwall is Hartland (32 miles, 52 km); straddling Devon and Somerset is the Exmoor coastline; the West Dorset Heritage Coast is some 25 miles (40 km) in length, and Purbeck 32 miles (52 km).

AREAS OF OUTSTANDING NATURAL BEAUTY

There are currently 43 Areas of Outstanding Natural Beauty (AONBs) in England and Wales. AONBs in the West Country include the Quantock Hills (38 sq miles, 99 sq km), England's first AONB, Dorset (399 sq miles, 1036 sq km), North Devon (66 sq miles, 171 sq km), South Devon (128 sq miles, 332 sq km), East Devon (102 sq miles, 267 sq km), the Mendip Hills (79 sq miles, 206 sq km), Cornwall (103 sq miles, 957 sq km) — a fragmented AONB — and the Isles of Scilly (6 sq miles, 16 sq km).

The Tamar Valley and the Black Down Hills are both currently being considered for AONB status.

AONBs are precious landscapes whose distinctive character and natural beauty are so outstanding that it is in the nation's interest to safeguard them through a unique legal status that can stimulate special policies for controlling development and encouraging proper land management. A responsibility of care is left with local authorities and the rural community. Almost all AONBs cross several authority boundaries, and to encourage consistent policies and positive co-ordination the Countryside

Commission recommends the formation of Joint Advisory Committees involving the different local authorities *and* the AONBs' landowners, farmers, residents and conservation interests, the appointment of AONB Officers and the preparation of Statements of Intent. The West Country is, in the main, well served in this respect.

SSSIs, NNRs, ESAs and SPAs

In addition to, and often covering areas of, the above designations, there are many Sites of Special Scientific Interest (SSSIs) and National Nature Reserves (NNRs), designated by English Nature. English Nature is the statutory adviser to Government on nature conservation in England and promotes the conservation of England's wildlife and natural features.

In the South-West, over 500 SSSIs have been notified, covering over 247,000 acres (100,000 ha) of wildlife habitats, geological features and landforms. There are about thirty National Nature Reserves in the region managed by English Nature. The greatest concentration is in south-east Dorset, where six heathland reserves safeguard some of the best examples of this severely threatened habitat. Bridgwater Bay NNR in Somerset consists mainly of extensive intertidal mudflats that support large numbers of wildfowl and waders, and on the north Devon coast is Braunton Burrows NNR — an extensive sand-dune system. The Axmouth to Lyme Regis Undercliffs NNR on the south coast of Devon is a dramatic landslip area of great importance for its geology and wildlife. Other Reserves include limestone woodland at Ebbor Gorge on the Mendips, the distinctive south-western oakwoods of Yarner Wood on Dartmoor, and Golitha Falls alongside the River Fowey in Cornwall. The waters around Lundy Island in the Bristol Channel have been designated as Britain's first Marine Nature Reserve.

Two areas — West Penwith and the Somerset Levels — have also been designated as Environmentally Sensitive Areas (ESAs) (see Walks 2.17 and 3.19) by the Ministry of Agriculture. The Ministry has also declared that parts of (or all) Exmoor and Dartmoor will receive ESA status during 1992 and 1993 respectively.

On 11 March 1992 the Government also announced that the Exe Estuary will be classified as a Special Protection Area for birds. The range of coastal habitats here including intertidal flats and saltmarsh supports avocets, black-tailed godwits and other vulnerable species including Sandwich tern, Common tern and Little tern.

SELECTED WALKS IN THE WEST COUNTRY

The view eastwards from Wavering Down, the Mendip Hills Area of Outstanding Natural Beauty.

INTRODUCTION TO THE ROUTE DESCRIPTIONS

1. ACCESS (see page 171)

For all Dartmoor, on land registered as common there is now legal (*de jure*) public access, and on Exmoor and Bodmin Moor *de facto* access on most of the open moorland exists. Routes make the most of this situation, and also follow public rights-of-way and permitted paths. Some cross areas where access agreements or permitted paths have been negotiated. Local bye-laws and regulations affecting the commons and access agreement areas must be respected and, in particular, 'short cuts' should not be taken that could cause annoyance to local people.

Along the coast, from Minehead in Somerset to Poole in Dorset, matters are more straightforward. Nearly all the coastal walks featured in this book follow sections of the South West Coast Path — a National Trail. You may find that a path has been diverted officially, perhaps to allow a badly eroded section to recover, or to avoid a recent landslip, or where an improvement has been made to the public right-of-way network.

2. ASCENT

The amount of climbing involved in each route has been estimated from the Outdoor Leisure, Pathfinder, or Landranger Ordnance Survey maps and should be regarded as approximate only. In most route descriptions specific reference is made to the length and height of individual climbs. The nature of coastal terrain makes ascent information general rather than comprehensive.

3. CAR-PARKS

Most of the walks start from public car-parks. For other walks, parking arrangements are suggested to prevent indiscriminate parking, which can be a great nuisance to local people.

Car break-ins can occur anywhere, even in the countryside. The police advise you to take valuables with you, or leave them at home; items of value are no longer safe hidden from view in the boot. When parking your vehicle, remember that it is illegal to drive more than 15 yards (14 m) from the road on to the open moorland.

Please remember that some of the walks start and finish in popular tourist and day-visitor areas. Where possible, peak times should be avoided to minimize disappointment.

4. INTERESTING FEATURES ON THE ROUTE

The best position for seeing these is indicated both in the route descriptions and on the maps, by *(1)*, *(2)*, etc.

5. LENGTH

These are strictly 'map miles' estimated from the Outdoor Leisure, Pathfinder or Landranger maps; no attempt has been made to take into account any ascent or descent involved.

6. MAPS

The maps are drawn to a scale of 1 : 25 000 or 1 : 50 000 and all names are as given on the Outdoor Leisure, Pathfinder or Landranger maps. Field boundaries in particular should be taken as a 'best description'. The maps have been drawn, in the main, so that each map points to grid north. The scale of some small features has been slightly exaggerated for clarity. For easy cross-reference, the relevant Outdoor, Pathfinder and Landranger sheets are indicated on each map.

7. ROUTE DESCRIPTION

The letters 'L' and 'R' stand for left and right respectively. Where these are used for changes of direction, they imply a turn of about 90° when facing in the direction of the walk. 'Half-L' and 'half-R' indicate a half-turn, i.e. approximately 45°, and 'back half-L' or 'back half-R' indicate three-quarter turns, i.e. about 135°. PFS stands for 'Public Footpath Sign', PBS for 'Public Bridleway Sign' and OS for 'Ordnance Survey'.

To avoid constant repetition, it should be assumed that all stiles and gates mentioned in the route description are to be crossed (unless there is a specific statement otherwise).

8. STANDARD OF THE ROUTES

The briefest examination of the route descriptions that follow will show that the routes described cover a wide range of both length and difficulty; some of the easy routes at least can be undertaken by a family party, with care, at most times of the year, while the hardest routes are only really suitable for experienced fellwalkers who are both fit and well-equipped. Any walker who is contemplating following a route should make sure before starting that it is within their ability.

It is difficult in practice, however, to assess the difficulty of any route because it is dependent upon a number of factors and will in any case vary considerably from day to day, even during the day, with the weather. Any consideration of weather conditions must, of course, be left to the walker himself (but read the section on safety and weather first). Apart from that, it is probably best to attempt an overall assessment of difficulty based upon the length, amount of ascent and descent, problems of route-finding and finally, upon the roughness of the terrain. Bodmin Moor, Dartmoor and Exmoor are not mountainous, but they should never be underestimated; the going underfoot can be very

SYMBOLS USED ON ROUTE MAPS

□	Ruin
✕	Gate
ⅈⅇ	Bridge
₶	Waterfall
⋯⋯	No path
——	Path
===	Track
⊢	Stile
∿∿∿	Wall
▲	OS Trig. Point
✝	Church
■	Occupied building
△	Summit
🌢	Cliff
Ⓟ	Car park
⋯50⋯	Contour (metres)
△68	Spot height (metres)
🖦	Lighthouse
⌇⌇⌇	Disused railway
∿	River/stream

heavy. Each of the routes has been given a grading based upon a consideration of these factors. A general description of each grade follows:

Easy (1) Generally short walks (up to 6 miles/9.7 km) over moderately easy ground with no problems of route-finding except in poor visibility. Progress is mostly over fairly gradual slopes with some short sections of more difficult ground. The paths may, however, sometimes run near steep slopes such as quarry or cliff edges; care should be taken here and among the moorland clitter.

Moderate (2) Rather longer walks (up to about 10 miles/16 km) with some routes over paths, but where some involve more difficult route-finding across moorland. Tor summits will be reached with climbing over steeper and rougher ground.

More strenuous (3) Longer walks (10–14 miles/16–22 km) with prolonged spells of climbing. Some rough ground calling for good route-finding ability, particularly in poor weather conditions.

Very strenuous (4) Only for the few if trying to complete in one day, and they involve long distances.

The walks are arranged in order of increasing difficulty, so that Route 1 is the easiest and Route 27 the hardest. Finally, a summary of each walk is given at the head of each section with information on the distance, amount of climbing and any special difficulties that will be met along the way.

9. STARTING AND FINISHING POINTS

All but two of the routes are circular in order to avoid any problems with transport when the walk is completed. The location of each starting and finishing point is given by the number of the appropriate Landranger (1 : 50 000) map with a six-figure grid reference (see page 173); thus (55–854383) indicates a grid reference which can be found on Landranger Sheet No. 55.

10. TIME FOR COMPLETION

The usual method of estimating the length of time needed for a walk is by Naismith's Rule: 'For ordinary walking allow one hour for every 3 miles (5 km) and add one hour for every 2000 feet (600 m) of ascent; for backpacking with a heavy load allow one hour for every $2\frac{1}{2}$ miles (4 km) and one hour for every 1500 feet (450 m) of ascent.' However, for many this tends to be over-optimistic and it is better for each walker to form an assessment of his or her own performance over one or two walks. Naismith's Rule also makes no allowance for rest or food stops or for the influence of weather conditions.

1·1

CORNWALL

WEST PENWITH: THE BOTALLACK CROWN MINES

This very short, easy walk allows exploration of a profoundly moving landscape on a rugged coastline where people once laboured in hard conditions to win tin, copper and arsenic. The engine-houses of The Crowns remain as haunting monuments to that endeavour. Today, these and other extensive workings in the area create a place of strange and silent beauty.

ROUTE DESCRIPTION (Map 1.1)

From the car-parking area, with the wall of a long-ruined building on your L, and a chimney-stack dead ahead, go R along the track towards the redundant winding gear of Allen's Shaft on the R. Opposite here cut L among the ruins, and follow the track round to the R, passing another ruined wall. The path soon meets the Coast Path. Here swing round to the L in front of the group of ruins (1). On the L is a series of buddles, once used in the sorting of tin ore. Leaving the Coast Path, with the chimney-stack immediately on your L, cut down R along the path leading down to The Crowns engine-houses. These are now restored and deserve exploration.

Retrace your steps back up to the Coast Path and cut up the slope directly ahead to the L of the chimney-stack. At the top turn R, passing the flues, and go under the arch and then immediately L for the car-park.

1   *Botallack Mines*
    Botallack Mine is famous for its two engine-houses — The Crowns section of the mine — sited on a small ledge above the sea. The lower engine-house is unusual in that the stack was built within the corner of the building, perhaps because of the restricted space available at the site. This engine-house was built some time before 1846 and that of the whim, higher up, was built in 1860 for a new incline shaft. Both structures illustrate the ingenuity of Cornish mine engineers. The granite blocks used in their construction all had to be lowered down the cliff, as did the heavier engine parts.

STARTING AND FINISHING
POINT
From the B3306, St Just–St Ives road, on reaching Botallack (1¼ m/2 km) north of St Just, drive into the village (signed 'Count House Restaurant'). Follow the signs to the Count House, passing Manor House Farm (R). The lane soon becomes an unsurfaced track. Continue straight on, and parking can be found on R, just beyond the Count House Restaurant (203–364333).
LENGTH
1 mile (1.6 km)
ASCENT
One climb: ⅓ mile (0.5 km) return from Crown Mines — 131 ft (40 m).

The Crowns, Botallack Head.

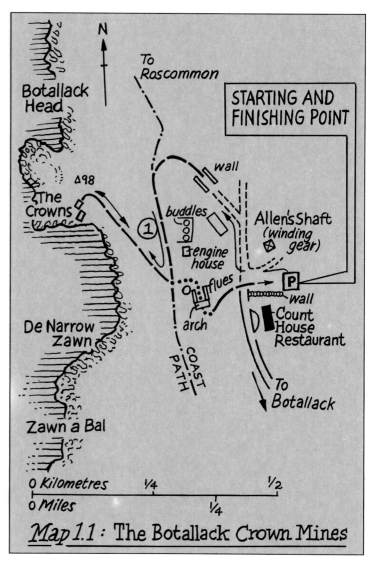

The galleries extended for $\frac{1}{3}$ mile (0.5 km) under the Atlantic. The lower engine-house shaft was the main pumping shaft and was sunk to the 135-fathom (810 ft/247 m) level. The upper engine-house is 110 ft (33 m) above sea level, and its diagonal shaft began at 30 ft (9 m) above sea level and inclined for a distance of 2500 ft (762 m). Above the cliffs was an extensive mine layout with eleven steam-engines in 1865, when 500 persons were employed. During its main period of operation from 1815 to 1914, the Botallack Crown Mine yielded 22,465 tons of copper, 124,888 tons of tin, and 1525 tons of arsenic. Most of the work, however, had come to an end in March 1895 due to low tin prices.

1·2

WEST DORSET

EGGARDON HILL

Sitting on Eggardon Hill is an Iron-Age hill-fort, spectacularly sited upon a high, windswept ridge of the Dorset uplands. The walk is included in this book by way of an introduction to the exhilarating experiences that can be gained from a walk over a hill-fort, of which there are many with public access in West Dorset, including Maiden Castle, Abbotsbury Hill-Fort, Lambert's Castle and Coney's Castle.

ROUTE DESCRIPTION (Map 1.2)

From the picnic area go back to the road junction, then turn L (signed 'Askerswell/Bridport'). At the next road junction continue straight on, passing the OS obelisk, which stands at 827 ft (252 m) above sea level. Continue down the lane for several hundred yards, and then turn R over a stile that leads on to a level footpath. At the end of this track, which offers fine views of the south-facing ramparts of the hill-fort, cross the stile on your L. The southern half of the hill-fort is owned by the National Trust; dogs must be kept on a lead when sheep are grazing.

    Follow the path running along the top of the lowermost rampart *(1)*. Within a short distance, landslips have interfered with the ramparts. Here cut across to the top rampart. The chalk downland turf supports many varieties of butterflies, including painted lady, brown argus, common and chalkhill blue, wall brown, marbled white and four species of skipper *(2)*. Skirt round the top of the hill-fort. The views are extensive and include the sea, and Dartmoor 53 miles (85 km) to the west. On reaching a wire fence, turn L over a wooden stile. The path then follows a dramatic ridge to a cliff-like outcrop of the spur — a haunt of buzzards and hawks — from which are more fine views west *(3)*.

    Retrace your steps back along the ridge, re-cross the stile, and continue straight on, keeping the fence on your L. After the uppermost rampart, cut half-R across the crest of the hill-fort. Follow the uppermost rampart round, and on reaching the fence turn R, then back over the stile to meet the track which returns

STARTING AND FINISHING POINT

From Bridport drive to Askerswell (4 miles/6.5 km east of Bridport). From the village centre, follow the minor lane for ½ mile (0.8 km) north-west to Spyway. At the road junction turn R. At the top of the hill, at the next T-junction, go straight on (signed 'Toller Porcorum'). Within 220 yards (200 m) go R (signed 'Wynford Eagle/Maiden Newton'). Park in the picnic area on the L (Dorset County Council) — Shatcombe Lane (194–549 948). The parking area is turfed; in wet weather please try to avoid wheel-spins.

LENGTH

2¾ miles (4.5 km)

ASCENT

Mostly level walking.

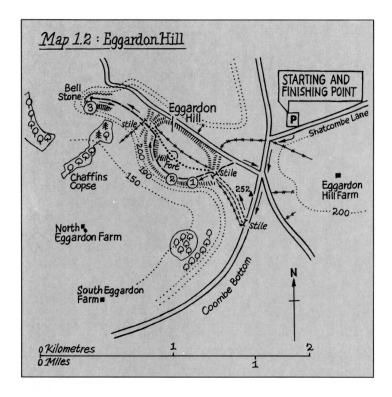

Map 1.2 : Eggardon Hill

Bell Stone
Eggardon Hill
stile
Chaffins Copse
Hill Fort
North Eggardon Farm
South Eggardon Farm
Coombe Bottom
STARTING AND FINISHING POINT
Shatcombe Lane
stile
252
Eggardon Hill Farm
200
stile
N

0 Kilometres   1   2
0 Miles   1

to the road. Within 16 yards (15 metres) along this track, go through the small, metal gate on the L, and follow the bridleway across the field. At the road go through the gate, and turn R for the return to Shatcombe Lane. Looking back, you have a superb view over the north-east ramparts of Eggardon.

1   *Eggardon hill-fort*
This spectacular, triple-banked, Iron-Age hill-fort is situated on a spur of chalk downland and dates from about 300 BC. Further rampart additions were made some time around 50 BC. It covers an area of 47 acres (19 ha). The southern half of the hill-fort was acquired by the National Trust in 1978. The northern part was unfortunately ploughed in the early 1970s, causing some damage.

The many depressions (over 160) inside the hill-fort are the sites of pits. Excavation of these has revealed that they were cut into the clay-with-flints subsoil to store grain. The large number of pits suggests a huge grain-storage capacity, reflecting the importance of Eggardon as an economic and administrative centre for the West Dorset chalkland. Eight circles, some 30 ft (9.1 m) in diameter, indicate the sites of huts. Four Romano-British field boundaries cross the hill.

Looking south from Eggardon Hill towards Haydon Down.

Enclosed by an eighteenth-century ditch and bank is an octagonal sea-mark 160 ft (48.7 m) across. It is believed that this was constructed around a clump of pine trees planted by Isaac Gulliver, a smuggler, as a navigation aid; the trees are long gone.

2 *Eggardon Hill*
Eggardon Hill is a Site of Special Scientific Interest and has one of the characteristic western variants of sheep's fescue dominated grassland. Devil's bit scabious and betony grow on south-west slopes. The south-facing embankments support a rich plant community, and here the hairy-stemmed, yellow-flowered, rough hawkbit is abundant. Scientific sampling has also revealed fourteen species of weevil.

3 *Hardy Country*
The hill has been claimed to be the Norcombe Hill of Thomas Hardy's *Far from the Madding Crowd*. 'Norcombe Hill . . ., one of the spots which suggest to a passer-by that he is in the presence of a shape approaching the indestructible as nearly as any to be found on earth'. It was here that a young sheepdog, half-trained, chased 200 ewes over the edge of a chalk pit to their deaths — 'The savings of a frugal life had been dispersed at a blow; his (Gabriel Oak's) hopes of being an independent farmer were laid low, possibly for ever'.

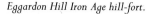

Eggardon Hill Iron Age hill-fort.

1·3

CORNWALL

ROCHE ROCK – TREZAISE – TRERANK

A short walk that includes the outstanding rock pile and rock-fast cell and chapel of Roche Rock, and which offers views of the interface between mid-Cornwall farming and the dominating china-clay industry. A surprising number of kissing-gates have to be negotiated — so take an appropriate partner!

ROUTE DESCRIPTION (Map 1.3)

From the lay-by take the path up to the rock pile and chapel, the latter built with raw solidity. Signs bring to your attention that Lord Falmouth allows public access to the Rock and its ruins, and to the grounds, entirely at visitors' own risk. Climbing and rock sampling are not allowed.

Metal ladders lead up through the cell and chapel to the summit. Take care on ascent and descent *(1)*. From the summit there are extensive views over Roche village and the devastated china-clay landscape *(2)*. From the base of the outcrop, below the ruin, turn R on to the small footpath and within a short distance head in a south-east direction on a smaller path through the gorse and bracken in the direction of the clay tips. At the stone stile, soon reached, look back for a full view of Roche Rock and the chapel. Cross the stile and follow the top R field hedgebank. Go through the kissing-gate into the next field and make for the kissing-gate directly ahead. Once through the gate, bear R (way-marked 'Public footpath Tresayes $\frac{1}{4}$'). Through another gate, follow the footpath towards the top L of the field. Negotiate another kissing-gate, and then follow the L field boundary. At the next kissing-gate there are fine views of Roche Rock. Continue on the footpath enclosed by stone hedgebanks to the lane at Tresayes (Trezaise). At the lane go R and on reaching the main road, go L passing an old chapel *(L)*. Follow the road for several hundred yards (metres) and, opposite Rock View Cottage, go R through the kissing-gate into the field and follow the public footpath (waymarked: 'Coldvreath $\frac{3}{4}$').

Keep to the R field hedgebank and go through the next kissing-gate. Bear half-L to the bottom field gate. On reaching the track

STARTING AND FINISHING POINT
Park in the small lay-by at Roche Rock on the Bugle road from Roche (200–991598). The turning is opposite the parish church. If the lay-by is full, park in the village and walk to the lay-by starting point.
LENGTH
$2\frac{1}{2}$ miles (4 km)
ASCENT
Mostly level walking. Short climb up metal ladders onto Roche Rock optional.

China-clay spoil tip, Hensbarrow Downs.

25

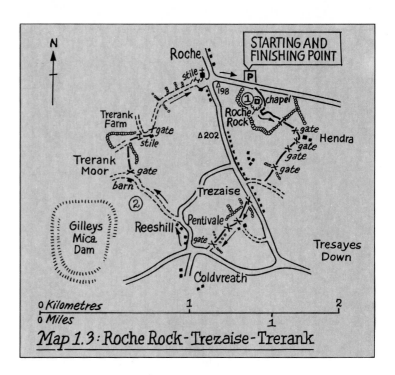

Map 1.3: Roche Rock-Trezaise-Trerank

between the cottages at Pentivale go R, passing a cottage and through a gate. Follow the L field hedgebank down, heading in the direction of two pylons. Through the next kissing-gate, cross over a small stream and at the road go R, then first R down the lane (signed: 'Nanpean/Whitemore').

Follow the lane down to the hamlet and here go along the track on your L, keeping a small stream close on the R. Keep on this track, passing a farm and cottage. This track soon becomes an unmetalled green lane. The currently worked china-clay tips contrast markedly with the lower re-colonizing tips. A barn is soon reached (L). Go through the gateway ahead into the field, ignoring the track which strikes off to the L just beyond the barn. Cross this field bearing half-R to its top corner. Enter the next field, going R for Trerank Farm on a well-defined path, one of many ancient church and field paths which crisscross the area. At Trerank Farm, go over the stile leading into the farmyard. Passing the farmhouse on your R, leave the farmyard by a wooden gate.

Continue straight on along the farm track with Roche Church now in view. The track soon becomes a metalled lane. When you reach the church, enter the ancient churchyard via the stone stile. Keep the church on your L and leave the churchyard via the main gateway. Cross straight over the road and continue down the lane for Roche Rock lay-by, or L down into the village if you are parked there.

1   Roche Rock

Roche Rock is a quartz-schorl dyke, brought about by the tourmalization of granite, and comprises three great rock piles. The central boss is the largest and has been locally referred to as 'Big Rock'.

The chapel was dedicated to St Michael and was licensed in 1409. Its dedication is shared with many churches, chapels and oratories in 'high places'. Below the chapel lay the cell of the chaplain, or earlier, as some believe, a hermit. This hermit may have been a leper, living here to avoid other people.

The legendary Tregeagle is said to have found sanctuary here with the hermit after abandoning the hopeless task set him to drain Dozmary Pool with a leaking limpet shell. His howling is heard when storm winds blow around the Rock.

2   China-clay production

China-clay is the result of kaolinization of granite — a process which probably occurred during the last of the hydrothermal alterations in the granite, largely brought about by the movement of acid solutions along joints. High-pressure water jets wash the clay from pit faces, and the overburden forms the characteristic waste tips — the Cornish Alps — which dominate so much of the St Austell area. China-clay is used in paper manufacture, some of it goes to the pottery industry, and it is also used in indigestion remedies and cosmetics.

Roche Rock and Chapel.

1·4

SOMERSET

BREAN DOWN

STARTING AND FINISHING
POINT
Car-park on the south side of
Brean Down, before the Tropical
Bird Garden (182–297586), 2
miles (3.2 km) to the west-south-
west of Weston-Super-Mare (8
miles/13 km by road). From
Weston-Super-Mare take the
A370 south following signs for
Bleadon. From the A370 at
Bleadon follow signs for Brean.
LENGTH
3 miles (4.8 km)
ASCENT
Two short, moderate ascents of
about 820 ft (250 m) in length: to
east Brean Down summit 230 ft
(70 m); to west Brean Down
summit 262 ft (80 m).

The bold limestone headland of Brean Down is a western outlier
of the Mendip Hills and is a major landmark of the Somerset
coast. This circular walk is full of wildlife and archaeological
interest. From it are unbroken views over Bridgwater Bay, the
Somerset levels dominated by Glastonbury Tor and Brent Knoll,
and to the south and south-east the uplands of Exmoor and the
Quantocks. Brean Down is owned by the National Trust (dogs
must be kept under proper control) and is a Site of Special
Scientific Interest due to its outstanding coastal/limestone habitats. The Down is managed and wardened by the National Trust
and Sedgemoor District Council with help from the Somerset
Trust for Nature Conservation.

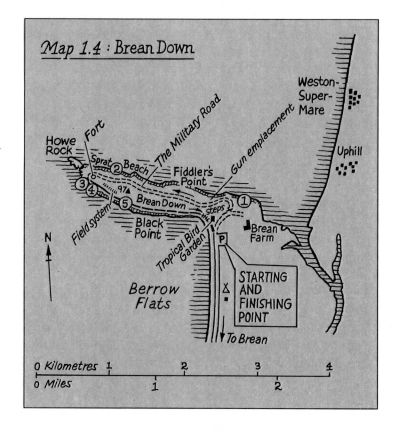

Opposite: across Weston Bay, dawn.

28

Brean Down Ridge.

ROUTE DESCRIPTION (Map 1.4)

From the car-park go along the track, keeping Brean Down Tropical Bird Garden on your L (waymarked: 'Public Footpath'). After skirting round the base of Brean Down for several hundred yards (metres), go L up the gated track and follow it up to the eastern summit of the Down *(1)*.

Follow the track round to the L, passing the World War II gun emplacements, which sit on the remains of an Iron-Age hill-fort, and pass a possible medieval pillow mound where rabbits would have been bred for food. Stay on the track — known as 'the Military Road' — which contours the north side of the Down almost to the westernmost end of the peninsula *(2)*. The massive nineteenth-century fort is soon reached. A notice here warns of dangerous structures and cliffs, but the ruins, without railings, can be explored with care *(3)*. Keeping the fort on your L *(4)*, walk up the slope to the summit on the south side of the Down passing later defences on the R. Walking on across the summit, the OS obelisk — at 318 ft (97 m) above sea level — is reached *(5)*. Continue across the summit and directly above the Bird Garden a flight of steps drops down to the base of the cliffs, allowing the return to the car-park.

1   *Brean Down*

Brean Down, and the islands of Steep Holm and Flat Holm, are extensions of the Mendip Hills. The Down comprises carboniferous limestone. About 290 million years ago these rocks were subjected to great movements in the earth's crust, which folded them in an east–west direction. This folding gave the Down the shape it is today.

2   *Local wildlife*

As far back as the Ice Age, arctic fox, reindeer and perhaps mammoth wandered on the Down. Today, it still supports a rich collection of plants and animals. The area is home to many birds, including resident skylarks, meadow pipits, rock pipits and stonechats. Thousands of birds frequent the area during spring and autumn migrations. House martins and swallows arrive in March and April, followed by swifts in early May, as well as wheatears, whitethroats and black caps. At the foot of the cliffs, the rock pipit is a regular breeder in small numbers, and small flocks of shelduck and mallard are often seen on the surrounding mudflats. Many limestone plant species are to be found. The rare white rock rose grows here, at its most northerly limit, in abundance.

3   *Nineteenth-century fort*

The fort was built in 1867 as a protection against possible invasion by Napoleon III. It is one of a chain of such forts on the Bristol Channel. Defended by seven 7-inch (18 cm) muzzle-loading cannons, it was blown up in July 1900 by a Gunner Haines, who fired his carbine into the ammunition store. Between 1905–1939 the fort was used as a café. It was re-fortified during World War II and was manned by 571 Regiment Coast Artillery Western Command.

4   *The Brean Down Harbour Company*

In 1861 the Brean Down Harbour Company was formed to construct a major port installation at the seaward end of Brean Down, with a direct link to the Bristol and Exeter railway line. It was hoped to provide a faster trans-Atlantic passenger service than that from Liverpool. The foundation stone was laid on 5 November, 1864, with great ceremony. Work continued sporadically, but the ill-fated project had been abandoned by the late 1880s. Nothing now remains.

5   *Archaeological remains*

The Down was an island before the Bleadon Levels were drained in medieval times for farming. For some 4000 years humans have lived, farmed, worshipped and defended here and these activities have left many visual remains of considerable archaeological interest — the whole of the Down is a Scheduled Ancient Monument.

1·5

SOMERSET

GLASTONBURY – CHALICE HILL – STONE DOWN HILL – GLASTONBURY TOR

STARTING AND FINISHING
POINT
Large, privately-owned car-park,
near Glastonbury Abbey on the
A39 (Magdalene Street), just
south of the Market Place in the
town centre (182–499388). Small
parking fee.
LENGTH
3 miles (6 km)
ASCENT
$\frac{1}{2}$ mile (0.8 km): Dod Lane–
Chalice Hill 131 ft (40 m); $\frac{3}{4}$ mile
(1.2 km): up Stone Down Lane
98 ft (30 m); $\frac{1}{2}$ mile (0.8 km): to
summit of Glastonbury Tor 177 ft
(54 m).

This short walk explores the remarkable Glastonbury area, the 'Avalon of the heart', the legendary origin of Christianity in Britain. Owing to the flatness of the surrounding levels, Glastonbury Tor is the focus of the landscape — a place of ancient sanctity and use, a place where the truth behind legend and myth depends on your own viewpoint and spirituality. Some lane and road walking.

ROUTE DESCRIPTION (Map 1.5)

From the car-park go R up Magdalene Street to the Market Place. The fourteenth-century gateway to Glastonbury Abbey is passed on the R (1). At the Cross turn R up High Street, passing The George and Pilgrims Inn on your L. Continuing in the same direction, you pass The Tribunal on the L, with its sixteenth-century front to a fifteenth-century building. This was formerly the Abbey Courthouse and was used by Judge Jeffreys during the Monmouth Rebellion Trials. Today it houses finds from the nearby Iron-Age Lake Villages (2). At the road junction at the top of High Street, just after Ye Queen's Head public house, turn R (highway signed: 'Frome/Shepton Mallet').

Opposite the gateway to the Abbey House, turn L up the road waymarked 'Public Footpath' (Dod Lane). Head up this lane and at the imposing early nineteenth-century Chalice Hill House (Ramala Centre) on the R, take the short off-shoot from the lane that leads up to a gate and iron stile. Go over the stile and continue on the footpath that leads up and over Chalice Hill (3). Glastonbury Tor, with its dominating church tower, soon comes into view.

At the end of the meadow go through the kissing-gate and turn L along Bulwarks Lane. Stay on the lane, skirting round the side of the hill. At the T-junction turn R along the lane. Where the lane bends to the R go straight on, ignoring the track leading off to the L. Continue on this green lane (locally known as Paradise Lane), keeping Glastonbury Tor on your R.

Cross a stile and follow along the gentle ridge. Go over the next stile encountered, and continue straight on (waymarked 'Public Footpath') keeping the field hedge on your L. From here you have a bird's-eye view over Higher Wick Farm (L). Almost at the end of the field turn L over a stile, and go straight on, keeping the field boundary on your L and barns over on your R. Look back for a glimpse of Glastonbury Tor before dropping down Stone Down Hill. Almost at the bottom of this field veer slightly to the R for a stile. Cross this stile and continue straight on (waymarked), keeping to the clear footpath leading to the bottom of the field. Here, above Wick Farm, cross the stile and bear R (waymarked) along the green lane. At the track T-junction, turn R uphill along Stone Down Lane. Some believe this to be an old processional path linking Glastonbury to Stonehenge, but it is more likely to be one of the many tracks and paths linking the surrounding countryside to the Abbey. Keep on this partially-metalled track over the hill and pass Stone Down bungalow (L). At the road junction go straight on, ignoring the lane dropping off to the L. Within a short distance go L through the concrete squeeze-stile for the National Trust's Glastonbury Tor estate. Sheep graze here, and dogs must be kept on leads. A made-up path leads up to the summit of the Tor. To help reduce erosion on the hill, the National Trust requests that visitors keep to the paths provided.

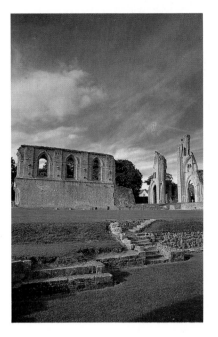

Glastonbury Abbey.

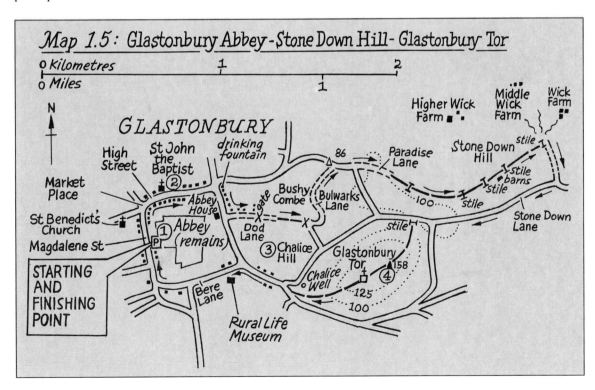

33

On the summit is a church tower — all that remains of St Michael's Church *(4)*. The view is breathtaking in all directions. From the church tower continue straight on, keeping to the concrete path, to drop down the dramatic south-western spur of Glastonbury Tor — an incongruous peak, with steep and sculptured slopes in a flat landscape. On reaching the lane turn R if visiting Chalice Well — a pre-Christian well consisting of two underground chambers about 9 ft (2.7 m) deep and associated with the legends of the Holy Grail. Otherwise go L and then R along the main road, staying on the raised pavement. At the roundabout go L down Bere Lane, passing the Rural Life Museum run by Somerset County Museums Service (open weekdays 10.00 am–5.00 pm; Saturdays and Sundays 2.00 pm–4.00 pm; small admission charge). The museum is housed in the Abbey Barn, which dates to about 1340. At the next major road junction, go R down Fishers Lane, which leads on to Magdalene Street and the return to the town centre. On approaching the Abbey car-park, to the R is a glimpse of the fourteenth-century abbot's kitchen, regarded as one of the best-preserved medieval kitchens in Europe.

1   Glastonbury Abbey
British Christianity was founded in Glastonbury in the first century AD. The first abbey here was probably a Celtic foundation of about AD 600, built around the site of St Mary's chapel. Dunstan, a local Saxon, started his work of Benedictine reform when he became abbot here in AD 944. His Abbey became the country's centre of learning. Its church was the chosen burial-place of the first kings of all England — Edmund, Edgar and Edmund Ironside, and it is also the legendary burial place of King Arthur.

For some 600 years the Abbey was the wealthiest in the country after Westminster, and it played a leading role in the spiritual, educational, cultural and national development of Great Britain until its dissolution in AD 1539. Because of its early foundation, Glastonbury became known as 'The Second Rome'. The abbey church was rebuilt after a fire which occurred in 1184. King Henry II regarded the fire as a national tragedy and appointed Ralph FitzStephen to rebuild it. When completed, just before its destruction some 350 years later, it was one of the longest churches in Europe.

Opening hours: Daily, except Christmas Day; 9.30 am–6.00 pm or dusk if earlier; opens 9.00 am June, July, August. Admission charge.

Glastonbury Tor and the tower of the ruined church of St Michael.

2 *Iron-Age remains*

Much of the peat moors surrounding Glastonbury lie below the level of the high Bristol Channel tides. The fen woodland on these levels and the peat bogs which replaced it were used for hunting during prehistoric times and were extensively settled. An artificial island, 'Lake Village', was built near the present town some time around 400 BC. This included some eighty-nine huts, which were occupied until Roman times. High-quality tools and ornaments were preserved in the peat and can be seen in The Tribunal. Water rose over the moors until the Glastonbury Abbey foundation began to develop the network of rhynes and banks that contribute to the present drainage system.

3 *The legend of the Holy Grail*

According to tradition, St Joseph of Arimathea introduced Christianity to Britain when he visited the area in about AD 64. He brought with him the cup or chalice from which the wine was drunk at the Last Supper, and buried it on Chalice Hill. The chalice is also known as the Holy Grail, the quest for which is a prominent theme surrounding King Arthur and the Knights of the Round Table.

4 *Glastonbury Tor*

Glastonbury Tor, a natural feature, is composed of layers of clay and blue limestone capped by a mass of hard, erosion-resistant sandstone. Its summit stands 518 ft (158 m) above sea level. The tower is all that remains of a medieval church dedicated to St Michael. This was built by the abbey to replace a previous church which fell in an earthquake in the thirteenth century.

Archaeological excavations over the summit area have revealed traces of fifth to sixth century buildings. Running along the hillside is a series of medieval strip lynchets. The tor has been a focus of legend, superstition and magic — some believe that the strip lynchets represent a 3-D maze, others that the hill has a hollow space inside. Some think that it has a secret entrance to the underworld.

1·6

SOMERSET

THE MENDIPS: COMPTON BISHOP — WAVERING DOWN — CROOK PEAK

A short walk by way of an introduction to the Mendips, offering superb views from the ridge top.

ROUTE DESCRIPTION (Map 1.6)

From the small pull-in opposite Rackley Lane go along the footpath (National Trust, waymarked). Within 16 yards (15 m) the path divides. Keep to the R-hand fork. Within a short distance you will see the entrance to a small cave on the L. Continue along the footpath through the trees to the next path junction and go straight on (waymarked: 'Compton Bishop'). Pass through the metal gate to leave the footpath.

Follow the track straight down to the lane to the unspoilt backwater village of Compton Bishop, and at the road junction go L passing Manor Farm (R), which possesses a series of fine, mullioned windows. St Andrew's Church is well worth a visit *(1)*.

Go down Church Lane and at the bottom of the hill cross the road and continue up the lane opposite. Follow this lane to its end in the small stableyard at the dwelling 'Glastonbury Thorn'. Continue straight on over the stile. Keep the field boundary on your R and follow along the bottom of this field, go through a gate and continue in the same direction and into the next field via a stile. Continuing on the same line, follow the edge of this field to a point about three-quarters of the way across where the footpath meets another path leading up from the R. Here, turn L to cut up the field to a high wall below a small wooded gully. Go over the stile, turn R and follow the path on the edge of the wooded area for a short distance until an obvious clear path cuts a way through the scrub growth (L). Go up this path, bearing half-R onto Wavering Down. The path is not clear in places, but traversing the hillside on the half-R line will bring you to a clump of yew trees near the summit of the Down.

STARTING AND FINISHING POINT
Small pull-in where Rackley Lane meets the road running between Loxton and Compton Bishop, 1.8 miles (3 km) west of Axbridge, 3.7 miles (6 km) east of Bleadon (182–398549). If this limited parking place is full, it will be necessary to park on one of several lay-bys between here and Webbington. If having to park in one of these lay-bys, walk down the road for the starting point. Please note that there is inadequate parking in Compton Bishop.

LENGTH
4 miles (6.4 km)

ASCENT
Three climbs: $\frac{1}{2}$ mile (0.8 km) ascent 328 ft (100 m) up south slope of Wavering Down; $\frac{1}{4}$ mile (0.4 km) ascent 167 ft (51 m) from Hill Farm to Wavering Down summit; $\frac{1}{4}$ mile (0.4 km) ascent 131 ft (40 m) to Crook Peak.

On the approach to the summit of Wavering Down there are good views across the gentle curve of hills above Compton Bishop. Keeping above the yew trees, Cheddar Reservoir comes into view on the R. Continue round the hillside on a clear path to Hill Farm. At Hill Farm, by the beech trees, turn L uphill keeping the drystone wall on your R. The route now follows part of the West Mendip Way (2). Now on the summit of Wavering Down, pass the OS obelisk 692 ft (211 m) above sea level and follow the curving ridge due west.

The route drops down over Compton Hill and then steadily ascends Crook Peak (696 ft/191 m), a landmark familiar to travellers up and down the M5, but how many have stood on its summit? The panorama from Crook Peak is a vast one, the height accentuated by the flat, low land to the south (3). Retrace your steps down the hill to the footpath junction by the stone wall. Here, turn R along a small grassy path that soon drops down through dense scrub into the combe leading back to Compton Bishop. Almost opposite the church the track divides. Take the R fork through the wood and keep on this path to reach the pull-in by Rackley Lane.

On Crook Peak.

1   *Compton Bishop church*
     Compton Bishop is situated in a hollow under the southern ridge of the Mendips. Compton Bishop (or 'Episcopi'), previous to its sequestration in the reign of Edward IV, was in

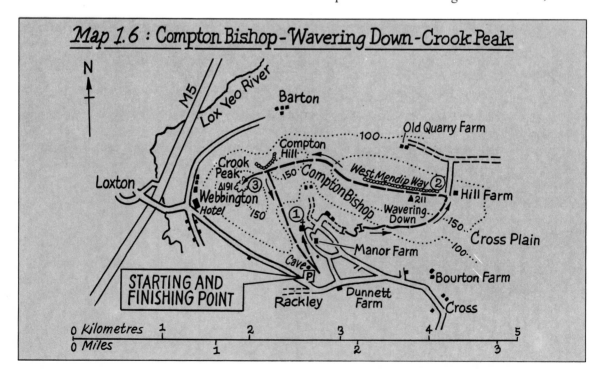

Map 1.6 : Compton Bishop – Wavering Down – Crook Peak

the possession of the See. The original church was of Saxon foundation and was dedicated to St Andrew later. The magnificent carved stone pulpit dates to the fourteenth century and is one of the best of its kind in Somerset. Slightly east of the south porch stands a fourteenth-century churchyard cross.

2 *The Mendip Way*

The 30-mile (48.2-km) long Mendip Way consists of a series of linked paths, utilizing public rights-of-way. It was devised and waymarked by the Rotary Clubs of Weston-Super-Mare, Wrington Vale, Mendip and Wells to commemorate Queen Elizabeth's Silver Jubilee in 1977. The route begins at Uphill, now virtually a suburb of Weston-Super-Mare and ends at Wells Cathedral.

3 *Crook Peak*

The rocky summit of Crook Peak is the most conspicuous landmark of the western Mendips. It was one of the chief Somerset beacon hills and was maintained for many years even before the Armada. The Churchwardens' Accounts at Banwell contain an entry for the year 1580: 'Pd. The firste daye of July for one load of wood for the beaken and for carrynge of the same to Croke Peke 0.5.0'. Crook Peak's prominent nature also makes it an important steering mark for ships in the Bristol Channel, and on Admiralty charts it was paradoxically called 'See-me-Not'.

Wavering Down and Crook Peak.

West Dorset

STONEBARROW HILL — UPCOT — GOLDEN CAP

A walk of great contrasts including undulating meadows, with areas of woodland, coastal landslips and dramatic cliffs – including Golden Cap, the highest point on the southern England coastline. Golden Cap is part of a large National Trust property that in total covers some 2000 acres (809 hectares).

ROUTE DESCRIPTIONS (Map 1.7)

With Lyme Bay on your R, continue along the summit of Stonebarrow Hill passing the National Trust Information Centre and shop (open Easter/May–October). Continue on the track and at the next path junction bear R (waymarked: 'Chardown Hill/St Gabriels'). Go through the gate and bear R again (waymarked: 'St Gabriels/Golden Cap'). The path cuts across a field in the direction of the flat-topped Golden Cap *(1)*. Cross over the next stile reached and skirt Chardown Hill, keeping on the track.

At the next gate bear R and stay on the track, which can be muddy in places, heading in the direction of the sea. Pass through another gate and, at the next path junction, continue straight on ('Bridleway: St Gabriels'). Pass Upcot Farm and by the barns turn L along the track (waymarked: 'St Gabriels Morcombelake'). At the next track junction go R ('St Gabriels $\frac{1}{2}$/Golden Cap'). This track drops down to cross a small stream and rises gently up to St Gabriel's. At the thatched holiday cottages go L (waymarked: 'Golden Cap $\frac{1}{2}$/Seatown $1\frac{1}{2}$'). The ruins of St Gabriel's Church (L) are soon encountered *(2)*. Stay on this bridleway up the hill, with Golden Cap on R.

Go through the next field gateway and cut R uphill on the north side of Golden Cap. Keep the field boundary on R. Almost at the top of this field, at the path junction bear L (waymarked: 'Bridleway Langdon Hill'). From here are fine inland views which take in the fir-crowned Langdon Hill, and the village of Morcombelake. Stay on the path, bearing R after the next gateway, keep the field boundary on your R. At the next junction turn R (waymarked: 'To Coast Path : Golden Cap'). Cross a stile and stay on the Coast Path over Golden Cap. A National Trust

STARTING AND FINISHING POINT

At the east end of Charmouth, leave the A35 at Newlands by the River Char, highway signed 'Stonebarrow (dead end)'. This is a narrow lane with infrequent passing places so proceed with care. A large car-park (National Trust) is reached on the top of Stonebarrow Hill (193–382 933).

LENGTH

4 miles (6.5 km)

ASCENT

Two short climbs: (250 m) up east flank of Golden Cap to summit — 164 ft (50 m); $\frac{1}{4}$ mile (0.4 km) from Westhay Farm to Stonebarrow Hill — 200 ft (61 m).

sign warns of unstable cliffs — people and dogs beware. An OS obelisk stands some 626 ft (191 m) above sea level — the highest point on the southern England coastline *(3)*. From this summit are superb views all round. Cross over the summit of Golden Cap, passing the Purbeck Stone monument 'Given by Members of the National Trust and friends in memory of the Earl of Antrim, KBE Chairman of the National Trust from 1966 until his death in 1977.'

Stay on the Coast Path down the west flank of Golden Cap, keeping St Gabriel's far below on your R. The cliffs here are unstable and small diversions in the Coast Path have been necessary. Cross through a large hedgerow and drop down towards St Gabriel's Mouth. The walk to the actual mouth, via a steep gully, is optional and at your own risk. In the combe, cross over a stile that leads into a field. Keep to the seaward field boundary above an area of naturally re-vegetating landslips (waymarked: 'Charmouth/Lyme Regis'). The route crosses the bottom of several fields via stiles. With Westhay Farm in full view, at the next path junction go straight on, keeping on the Coast Path (waymarked: 'Charmouth $1\frac{1}{2}$') ignoring the path on the R to Stonebarrow Hill and Morcombelake.

The Coast Path drops into a combe and crosses a stream (Ridge Water) via a footbridge. Go over a stile into the next field and bear R on the Coast Path. Cross Westhay Water via a footbridge. Leave the Coast Path near Westhay Farm, by going

Landslips and Lyme Bay from Golden Cap.

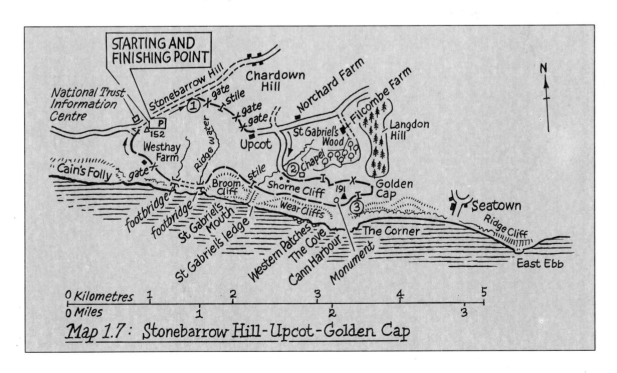

Map 1.7: Stonebarrow Hill–Upcot–Golden Cap

half-R (waymarked 'Westhay/Stonebarrow $\frac{1}{2}$'). Keep to the R of the farmhouse and go through the wooden gate to pick up a track leading up Stonebarrow Hill. Just beyond the farm drive entrance, on the bend, leave the track and continue straight up on the bridleway to Stonebarrow Hill. At the next grass track junction go R for the return to the car-park and a final view of Golden Cap.

1 *National Trust coastline*

Since the 1965 launch of Enterprise Neptune, the National Trust has had a policy of acquiring much of the unspoilt coastline in the area, as well as the traditional field patterns between Eype and Lyme Regis. The area comprises unimproved pastureland and lush meadows — a nineteenth-century landscape of small fields and dense hedgerows. The area is regionally and nationally important for the richness and variety of plants to be found including orchids, natural grasses and marsh flowers. Fertilizers and chemicals are applied on a very restricted basis, and optimum numbers of cattle are grazed to prevent encroachment by coarse grasses. Gorse is rotationally cut, or burned, to assist rejuvenation, providing a range of cover for birds and insects.

2 *Stanton St Gabriel*

Stanton St Gabriel (St Gabriel's) today comprises no more than a few buildings, but in 1650 twenty-three families were living around the green. The re-routing of the coastal road in 1825 brought about its isolation. The thirteenth-century St Gabriel's Church, now a ruin, was built as a chapel-of-ease to the mother church of Whitchurch Canonicorum. Services were last held there some time before 1800. The church was then believed to have been used as a receiving-house for smuggled goods, including silks, tobacco and kegs of brandy, for a short period. Ghost stories abounded to deter revenue men from investigating. Smuggling was brought to an end by stiffer penalties and the building of coastguard cottages at Seatown.

3 *Golden Cap*

Most of the cliffs skirting Lyme Bay, broken at intervals by small valleys, consist of a lower section of mainly Jurassic clays and shales and an upper layer formed from Cretaceous sandstone. Both Golden Cap and Stonebarrow Hill have this structure. The resistant greensand 'cap' sits on top of the softer, more erosive clays that are particularly prone to landslip.

Golden Cap — the highest point on the southern England coastline.

1·8

CORNWALL

ROSELAND PENINSULA: PORTH FARM — ST ANTHONY HEAD — PLACE — NORTH HILL POINT

STARTING AND FINISHING POINT

Follow the A3078, which leaves the A390 mid-way between Truro and Probus (highway signed 'St Mawes'), for 10 miles (16 km) to Trewithian. From here head due south passing Portscatho and follow St Anthony road. Narrow lanes — approach with care. Park in one of the two small National Trust car-parks at Porth Farm (204–868329); or if full, continue on to St Anthony Head National Trust car-park (204–848 312).

MAPS

OS Pathfinder 1 : 25000 1366 Falmouth and St Mawes recommended.

LENGTH

$5\frac{1}{2}$ miles (8.75 km)

ASCENT

Mainly level walking.

This delightful walk is a circuit of the southern end of the Roseland Peninsula. It offers extensive views of the Carrick Roads — a huge natural harbour for Falmouth, and includes the more intimate landscape of the Percuil River and several of its creeks.

ROUTE DESCRIPTION (Map 1.8)

From the car-park at Porth Farm, cross the road and follow the track waymarked 'To the Beach', passing underneath a farm building. From the sandy Towan Beach turn R on to the Coast Path. Continue on the Coast Path, passing through a kissing-gate. The path skirts around Killigeran Head with good views back over Towan Beach and Greeb Point, and to the north-east across Gerrans Bay to Nare Head and Gull Rock, and across Veryon Bay to Dodman Point. Pass Porthmellin Head.

Bohortha village can be seen ahead as you pass Elwinick Cove. The Coast Path continues above Porthbeor Beach, where huge swells from the Atlantic come rolling in. Drake's Down and Zone Point are seen ahead. Go over the stile at the end of the National Trust's Porthbeor estate. A good stretch of level clifftop walking is followed by a short, steep climb on the approach to Zone Point (National Trust).

On approaching St Anthony Head, you come to St Anthony Battery. After passing the National Trust's holiday cottages on the R, stay on the Coast Path by turning L and dropping down the steps to the lighthouse. The public are advised that a fog signal emitting a very loud noise may be sounded in this vicinity at any time, without prior warning (1). From the lighthouse retrace your tracks to the bottom of the steps, and then continue on the lower Coast Path passing the former Paraffin Store for the lighthouse (L). To the north Great Molunan and Carricknath Point headlands can be seen. The route leaves the National Trust's property, and continues along a boardwalk across an old dam, where an optional path leads down to the beach at Great Molunan. The Coast Path then skirts round north-eastwards towards Amsterdam Point *(2)*, offering views across St Mawes Harbour to St Mawes Castle and the village.

Cross a stile and keep to the lower side of the field until reaching the woodland ahead. At the woodland boundary turn R uphill (Coast Path waymarking). After a short, steep climb go over the stone stile (waymarked). Keep to the L field boundary and, at the bottom of the field, turn L over the stile and bear R along the track. Keep on the Coast Path forking to the R of an entrance to Place House (private) *(3)*. Go uphill and the Coast Path then skirts round to the L and passes through St Anthony churchyard *(4)*. Leave the churchyard via a stone stile and turn L down the lane (waymarked: 'Coast Path Place Quay'). A few waders may be seen here, including oystercatcher, curlew and redshank. From Place Quay go over the stile and turn R along the public footpath waymarked: 'Porth Farm 1½ miles'. This path keeps to the bottom of the field, and provides a wonderful view of St Mawes. At the end of the field, the path enters the National Trust property of Drawler's Plantation via a kissing-gate. Follow the path through the plantation.

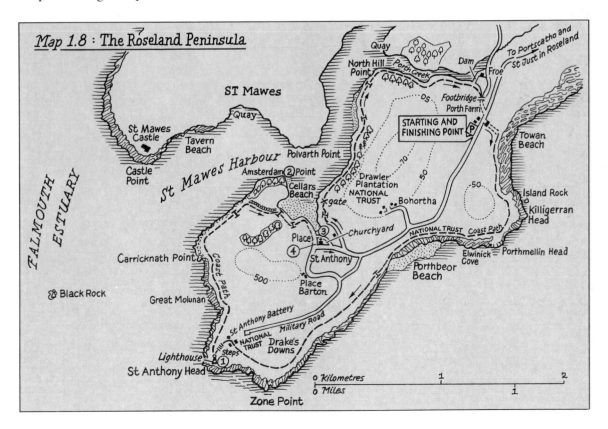

Ignore the public footpath on the R waymarked: 'To Bohortha', and go straight on to enter another field via a stile. At the far end of this field go over the stile to enter the woodland on North-hill Point. The path then skirts above Porth Creek. Ignore the next footpath on the R to Bohortha Farm. Keep straight on, noticing several rotting wooden hulls in the creek. Leave the woodland via the stile, keep straight on, and at the bottom of the field cross the footbridge at the head of the creek. Go R along a broad path running parallel to the lane for the return to Porth Farm.

Opposite: Porth Creek, Froe.

1   *St Anthony Lighthouse*
St Anthony Lighthouse was built in 1835 and is now fully automated. It is open to visitors on an irregular basis. Its light is visible for 14 miles (22.5 km) and shows red in the direc-

St Just-in-Roseland church.
Although not on the walk, it is not far away and well worth a visit whilst on the Roseland peninsula.

tion of the Manacles (Church Rocks) — a group of sub-merged and half-submerged rocks that have claimed many ships.

When the lighthouse was first built, a bell was rung every minute to warn of fog. This was replaced in 1954 by a nautophone.

2   *Coastal wildlife*

The sandy and rocky shoreline north-east from Carricknath Point is of outstanding importance for its marine life, including sea-anemones, sea urchins and burrowing shellfish and molluscs. Roseland Voluntary Marine Conservation Area, which covers the eastern shores of Carrick Roads up to St Just, was set up in 1982 to help conserve and protect the marine wildlife communities. Carrick District Council is establishing a database on the whole of the estuary and river complex.

3   *Place House*

Place House stands on the site of a small Augustinian priory built in the twelfth century by monks from Plympton. After the dissolution of the monasteries in the sixteenth century, the stones were taken by barge to St Mawes for use in the building of the castle. A large house was built on the site of the priory and in the mid-seventeenth century this was acquired by the Spry family. Extensive Victorian rebuilding left little of this original house. During World War II it was commandeered by the Royal Navy, and for a period shortly after the war it was a home for displaced Europeans. In 1949 it was converted into a holiday camp; it then became a hotel. Since 1982 it has reverted back to private use in the name of Spry.

4   *St Anthony's Church*

When the Augustinian priory was dissolved, the nave of the twelfth-century church was saved because it had been used for public worship. The south doorway is Norman, but following the rebuilding of Place House in the nineteenth century the chancel was rebuilt to match the medieval one. A tower was added to imitate the one on the house. At the time of writing the church was in need of more care. Inside is a fine roof and a fine series of memorials to the Spry family. During the eighteenth and nineteenth centuries members of this family achieved distinguished naval careers. There is also an interesting memorial to Lieutenant Thomas Wilks — who was for many years the signal officer at St Anthony Head. He died on 30 April, 1823, and 'In his general intercourse with society, he illustrated the saying of the poet, that ''An honest man is the noblest work of God'' '.

2·9

CORNWALL

WEST PENWITH: PORTH CURNO — ST LEVAN — TREEN — PENBERTH — TRERYN DINAS

This walk of moderate length explores a southern portion of the Penwith peninsula, which displays a great variety of scenery. An inland start to the route (involving some $1\frac{1}{4}$ miles/2 km of lane walking) allows an outstanding return coastal walk from the timeless fishing village of Penberth, then over the dramatic promontory of Treryn Dinas to Porthcurno. Dogs are prohibited on Porth Curno beach.

ROUTE DESCRIPTION (Map 2.9)

From the bottom end of the car-park go to the beach (waymarked). Porth Curno is a superb, steeply shelving beach but is very hazardous for swimming because of strong currents. From the head of the beach go R (Coast Path waymarking: 'Porthgwarra'). The Coast Path skirts around Minack Point. A sign before embarking on this stretch draws attention to an alternative route leading off on the R to a point above the Minack Theatre. This is because the lower Coast Path to Minack involves a difficult ascent, and is not recommended for young children or elderly persons. Stay on the lower path if you feel adventurous, keeping the Minack Theatre on your R. Those taking the alternative route turn R up the steep path leading to a surface track. From here follow the waymarking for Minack Theatre. At the car-park go R through the kissing-gate to continue on the Coast Path *(1)*.

The Coast Path then crosses Pedn-mên-an-mere (National Trust) ('the rocky headland by the sea'), which again offers a superb view to the east. At the next path junction go straight on, ignoring the track on the R. Above Porth Chapel cross the stream. You are requested to keep dogs on a lead and under control. The Coast Path climbs up to St Levan Holy Well *(2)*. From here leave the Coast Path by going R on a footpath up the valley leading to St Levan village. St Levan church soon comes into view on the R. On approaching the village, cross the stream

STARTING AND FINISHING POINT
Large fee-paying car-park at Porthcurno (203–384225) 8 miles (13 km) south-west of Penzance via the B3283 through St Buryan and Treen to Trethewey — follow this twisting road with care.
RECOMMENDED MAP
OS Pathfinder 1 : 25 000 Sheet 1368 Lands End and Newlyn.
LENGTH
5 miles (8 km)
ASCENT
Two short coastal ascents: Minack Point–Pedn-mên-an-mere or Minack Theatre car-park; Penberth Cove up on to Cribba Head.

and go through the gate. After exploring the church, leave the top end of the churchyard via a granite grid-stile; continue straight on up the field to the stone stile ahead and cross it. Go straight across the middle of the next field, passing a low granite cross on the L. On approaching Rospletha make for the L of the house. From here follow the broad track leading into Porthcurno.

At the road in Porthcurno cross straight over and go through the gap in the wall to pass a row of garages on your R. Just above the main building of the Cable and Wireless Telecommunications College, go L up the stony track (waymarked: 'Footpath'). This soon becomes a narrower path, which in turn divides. Take the L fork, passing a group of telecommunication aerials. Cut across the middle of the next three fields heading towards Trendrennen. Cut between the farm buildings and the cottages and go L up a track and then immediately R over a stone stile. Bear half-L across the field (crops may be growing here — use common sense). Go over the stone stile at the corner of the field, St Buryan church tower and the domed hills of Carn Brea and Bartinney Downs are seen to the L when crossing the next field. Leave this field by the gateway and keep on the same line, following a short length of field boundary to another gateway/stile. Maintain the same line across another field, go over the stone stile and from this point head for Treen village, crossing two more fields. At the edge of the village follow the track (often muddy) to the surfaced lane. In Treen go L along the lane passing Treen Farm (R) and the Logan Rock public-house (L). At the road junction turn R and then immediately R down the lane to Penberth.

Follow the lane down to Penberth Cove (National Trust) *(3)*. From the granite slipway go R (waymarked: 'Coast Path'). A steep climb then follows up over Cribban Head. The Iron-Age cliff castle of Treryn Dinas, comprising a series of ditches and ramparts across the isthmus, is soon reached. Here turn L on to the path which leads towards the Logan Rock *(4)*. It is possible to go round much of the headland in a clockwise direction.

Return to the Coast Path and stay on it to the next path junction. Turn L here along the public footpath that skirts Treen Cliff edge (National Trust) for dramatic views back to Treryn Dinas. A public footpath leads off from the L down to the base of the cliffs to Pednevounder Beach (check the tide tables, for this is one of Cornwall's finest beaches). The route down and back up requires some nerve, and is therefore optional. Continue along the cliff path, past a National Trust cairn, until it rejoins the

Logan Rock and Horrace from Pedn-mên-an-mere.

Coast Path on Carn Kizzie. Pass the pill-boxes and shortly after go over a stone stile (waymarked: 'Coast Path'). The Coast Path then passes over Percella Point and gives good views over Porth Curno. Stay on the Coast Path for the return to the beach and car-park.

1   *The Minack Theatre*

The Minack Theatre is set in a natural amphitheatre halfway down the cliff face, not so dissimilar to the Greek and Roman cliff theatres. During the summer, open-air plays are performed. The theatre was founded by Miss Rowena Cade in 1932. She died in March 1983, aged 89.

2   *St Levan*

The village of St Levan is named after the saint of that name, believed to be a Celtic saint who landed at what is now known as Porth Chapel. The Holy Well of St Levan and the Baptistry are connected to the remains of a small chapel on the cliff edge lower down by a flight of about fifty stone steps. The steps were uncovered as a result of excavations carried out in 1931.

The date of the first church is not known — the present church may well stand on the shrine of St Levan. The north transept is thirteenth century; the rest of the building,

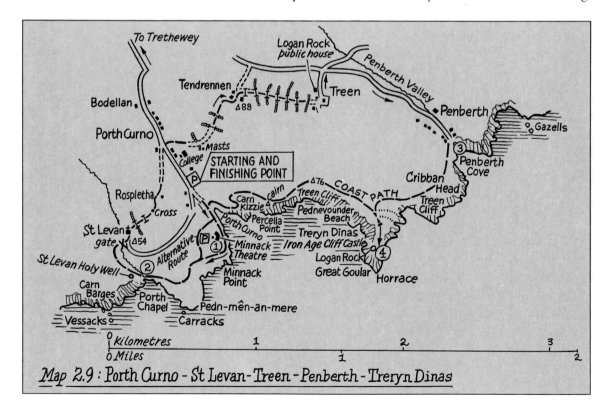

Map 2.9: Porth Curno - St Levan - Treen - Penberth - Treryn Dinas

Penberth Cove.

including the tower, porch, nave and south aisle, are fif-teenth century. The fifteenth-century bench ends are worth examining — one represents two fish, one on a hook, depicting a legend associated with the saint. Others show a shepherd with a crook, profiles of medieval parishioners, two eagles and a jester with cap and bells.

3   *Penberth*
The small fishing hamlet of Penberth is totally unspoilt — no commercialism here. Cottages, a granite slipway and a superb capstan remain unviolated. The National Trust has a policy to let the cottages to working families with businesses in the valley.

4   *The Logan Rock*
The Logan Rock, weighing over 65 tons, is perched high on a rock support on the dramatic promontory of Treryn Dinas. By the nineteenth century the stone had attracted visitors from Britain and Europe. On 8 April, 1824, Lieutenant Hugh Colvill Goldsmith (nephew of the writer, Oliver Goldsmith), with some of his crew from HMS *Nimble*, dis-lodged the rock, making it fall into a crevice below. His actions caused a great outcry, and local guides lost their income. To put right the 'indescrete folly', capstans, tim-bers, blocks and chains were landed in October in the same year to replace the rock. The Logan Rock, in the presence of thousands, was replaced at 4.20 pm on Tuesday, 2 November, 1824.

2·10

DEVON

DARTMOOR: MERRIVALE — HUCKEN TOR — SWELL TOR — KING'S TOR

STARTING AND FINISHING POINT
Car-park in a roadside quarry on the L side of the B3357 as you approach Merrivale Bridge from Princetown; 8 miles (5 km) west of Two Bridges, $4\frac{1}{2}$ miles (7.2 km) east of Tavistock (191–553750). See also OS Outdoor Leisure 28 (1 : 25 000) — Dartmoor.
LENGTH
$5\frac{1}{2}$ miles (8.75 km)
ASCENT
Mostly level walking. Two $\frac{1}{4}$-mile (0.4-km) climbs — from crossroads to Criptor farm track, 164 ft (50 m), and from Criptor to railway trackbed 230 ft (70 m).

The route offers wide views of the beautiful wood-and-torscape of the River Walkham valley. It follows for much of its moorland length the now-closed Yelverton to Princetown railway, which was built in 1881 along the trackbed of an earlier line — a horse-track tramway (the Plymouth and Dartmoor Railway) — used for transporting granite from nearby quarries. The walk ends with an exploration of the prehistoric stone rows, stone circles, cairns and standing stones on Long Ash Hill, which together represent one of the finest groups of ancient monuments on Dartmoor.

ROUTE DESCRIPTION (Map 2.10)

From the west end of the car-park walk down the road towards the River Walkham valley. Great Mis Tor is seen to the R, and ahead the view is dominated by Merrivale Quarry — the only surviving working quarry on Dartmoor. Turn L at Hillside and continue along the bridlepath (waymarked: 'Bridlepath to rd. Daveytown $1\frac{1}{2}$ km'). Across the valley (half-R) stands Vixen Tor. This spectacular rock-pile of ramparts and bastions is the highest tor on Dartmoor from the ground to its top — 93 ft (29.3 m) on its south face (1).

At Longash Farm continue on the bridlepath (waymarked), passing through a gate. Dogs must be kept on a lead through the farmyard. Go straight through the farmyard, closing the gates behind you. The bridlepath soon enters Longash Wood. Within a short distance a stream is crossed by a small, plant-covered clapper-bridge. Follow the well-defined track skirting above the Walkham valley. The low profile of Hucken Tor, moss-covered and tree-shaded, is reached next. This is a remarkable, haunting place in which to linger. The bridlepath continues on through a wooden gate between two outcrops of the tor. Continue on the track, passing through several gates, to reach a narrow, metalled lane. Go down this lane, passing Daveytown (L) and Withill (L). A gradual climb then leads up to the crossroads.

At Criptor Cross go L up the dead-end lane (steep ascent). Cross the cattle-grid and continue straight on along the track running below Ingra Tor (R) (ignore the track leading off to the R). King's Tor, Swell Tor and North Hessary Tor mast are seen directly ahead. Keeping on the track, pass through a gate, and continue straight on to the point where the track bends to the L to Criptor. Keep straight on and once across the stream go R along the waymarked bridlepath. The path becomes ill-defined over this stretch of rough moorland, but bear half-L, crossing a stream, and head uphill keeping a stone wall on your L. Occasional blue waymarking spots on rocks mark the way up to a small gate in the wire fence ahead. Go through the gate and then turn L along the trackbed of the disused Yelverton and Princetown Railway, which was built for most of its length on the earlier Plymouth and Dartmoor Railway *(2)*. Follow the railway for

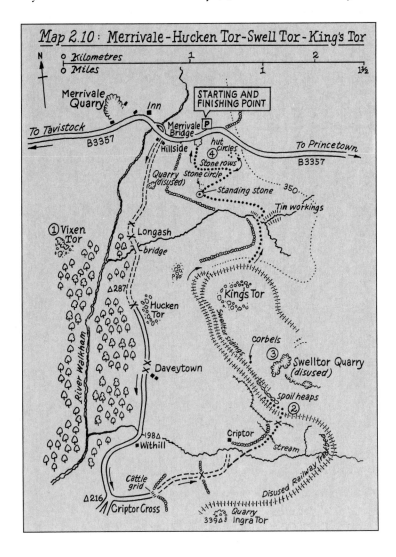

In Longash Wood, the Walkham Valley.

several hundred yards (metres) and at the point where the fencing (L) ends, cut R, and with care go over a small area of spoil heaps. You come out by a ruined building opposite the entrance to Swell Tor Quarry. The area deserves exploration *(3)*.

At the ruined building turn L along the trackbed of Swell Tor Sidings, on which remain some wooden sleepers with protruding bolts (watch your feet!). Abandoned, worked granite litters the siding, and you pass twelve granite corbels (R), which were cut out in the early 1900s for the new London Bridge but which were obviously surplus to requirements.

Where the sidings trackbed meets the main railway trackbed continue straight on over a well-constructed granite bridge. Skirting King's Tor the trackbed divides. The cutting ahead is the line of the Yelverton–Princetown Railway; to the L is the line of the Plymouth and Dartmoor Railway. The route follows the latter, which skirts around the hillside and from it are extensive views over the Walkham valley and beyond to Bodmin Moor. Stay on the trackbed, which soon re-unites with the later railway. At the point where the railway bears R, and with Yellowmeade Farm and North Hessary Tor mast in view ahead, leave the railway and go down the slope (L) through the clitter to the corner of a stone wall. Follow the wall round for a short distance and cross a stream (the Pila Brook) via a small ford (half-R). If the waters run deep, it is possible to cross further upstream. Follow the path directly ahead and once above the tin workings go L, heading for a solitary, prehistoric standing stone to the R of the stone wall. This stone stands some 10 ft 4 in (3.1 m) high. From this menhir, go R to the small, prehistoric stone circle ahead. From here bear half-R to the easternmost end of the stone rows. This prehistoric sanctuary on Long Ash Hill represents one of the finest groups of ancient monuments on Dartmoor *(4)*.

Looking down the stone rows, to the R are a number of hut circles — the foundations of prehistoric homes — and these deserve exploring. Then walk down between the stone rows, if you are lucky with a setting sun ahead, passing several kistvaens on route. From the blocking stones at the western end of the stone row turn R down the hill to the car-park.

1   Vixen Tor

Legend claims that Vixen Tor was the home of the evil witch, Vixana. Calling down a mist, she would lure travellers into the nearby mire where they would meet their deaths. A young man who had the ability to see through the mist, and who owned a ring that could make him invisible, became a

Prehistoric stone rows on the level plain of Long Ash Hill, Merrivale.

hero overnight when he killed the witch. As he approached the mire disguised as a traveller, she summoned the mist upon him but, as the mist cleared, he was nowhere to be seen from her position on top of the tor. He crept up silently behind her and, unseen, he gave a push . . .

2 *The Plymouth and Dartmoor Railway*

The Plymouth and Dartmoor Railway (P & D R) was the brainchild of Sir Thomas Tyrwhitt, private secretary to George, Prince Regent. In 1819 he submitted a tramroad plan to Plymouth Chamber of Commerce, and Royal Assent for this horse-driven railroad was given in 1821. This was to be Devon's first iron railroad and was opened on 26 September, 1823. It ran from Foggintor (Royal Oak) Quarries, and soon after from Princetown itself, to Crabtree Wharf on the Laira estuary just to the east of Plymouth — a distance of 25 miles (40.2 km). The tramway had a gauge of $4\frac{1}{2}$ ft (1.4 m) and iron rails were bolted to granite sets. The subsequent Yelverton to Princetown branch line was never profitable and closed on 5 March, 1956.

3 *Swell Tor Quarry*

The development of the quarries was closely associated with the construction of the P & D R, and production continued at a high rate, although not continuously, during the nineteenth century. Towards the end of the century, the centre of attention was turned to Swell Tor. Work continued on a large scale until World War I. About ninety men were employed there at that time.

4 *Prehistoric remains on Long Ash Hill*

The prehistoric monuments on the level plain of Long Ash Hill appear to be a prehistoric sanctuary used for burials and ceremonies by several generations. Two double stone rows set 30 yards (27.4 m) apart run parallel to each other in an almost east–west orientation. These rows thus form a prehistoric 'avenue'. The northern row is 180 yards (164.6 m) long and about 160 stones are remaining. The southern row consists of over 200 stones and roughly midway along it is a cairn marked by a circle of stones. A third row is single and 45 yards (41 m) long, being orientated west of south and from this may be the traces of another row.

Associated with the rows are a number of small cairns and exposed kistvaens — one kistvaen having had its coverstone split in 1860 to yield a gate-post. The nearby stone circle is some 62 ft (19 m) across and eleven stones are remaining.

2·11

WEST DORSET

ABBOTSBURY — CHESIL BEACH — ABBOTSBURY CASTLE

This walk of moderate length takes in much of prehistoric and medieval interest. It includes an outstanding ridge walk and one of the most interesting and enigmatic stretches of the Dorset coastline — Chesil Beach. Walking on the shingle here can be arduous but rewarding.

ROUTE DESCRIPTION (Map 2.11)

From the car-park cut through to the parish church of St Nicholas via the churchyard. On the south side of the church stand the ruins of the Abbey Church of St Peter *(1)*.

From the churchyard go L along the lane. A large pond is passed on the L and ahead is a large, thatched tithe barn *(2)*. From the barn follow the lane in the direction of the fifteenth-century St Catherine's Chapel, which crowns Chapel Hill. After about 100 yards (metres) go R down a surfaced track (signed: 'Swannery — Pedestrians — No Cars Please'). Pass several cottages on route to the Swannery car-park. From the car-park go R over a stile and walk along the private road leading to the Swannery. Dogs are not allowed, and visitors are asked to keep on this road to avoid disturbing wildfowl. Keep to a small stream on your R and you soon reach an area of pollarded willows, also on the R.

Here, by the willows, go over the stream via a small foot-bridge (stone waymark: 'Sub-tropical gardens'). Continue straight on up the path leading into and out of a field via stiles. Then go half-R (fingerpost waymarking: 'Tropical Gardens'). Head for and pass the pill-box on the side of the hill. The north-west end of The Fleet is now in view, an area of water impounded between a shingle beach and the old inland coastline *(3)*. Go through the next gate and stay on the Coast Path, keeping the fence line on your L. Ahead are Abbotsbury Gardens, and to the R is Wear's Hill ridge. At a wide track go over the stile and bear R (waymarked: 'Chesil Bank/West Bexington'). This track can be muddy in places. At the end of the track go through the gate — mud and earth give way to the shingle of Chesil Beach.

STARTING AND FINISHING POINT
Abbotsbury, 8 miles (13 km) north-west of Weymouth on the B3157. Large car-park by Abbotsbury church at east end of village (194–578853). An alternative parking area is available to the south of Abbotsbury Gardens (194–560847).
LENGTH
$6\frac{1}{4}$ miles (10 km)
ASCENT
One climb: $\frac{3}{4}$ mile (1.2 km) Chesil Beach to Tulk's Hill summit — 590 ft (180 m)

Opposite: access provision for the disabled and less mobile onto the shingle ridge, Chesil Beach.

Turn L up onto the shingle ridge and continue along the ridge north-west in the direction of the flap-topped Golden Cap *(4)*. The shingle has a wilderness quality all of its own, but can be tiring to walk on. Stay on the ridge, passing a row of cottages (R), and at about 380 yards (350 m) before reaching the next row of cottages, leave the beach by going R across a narrow road up a bridlepath (waymarked: 'Abbotsbury Hill Fort'). Walk up the field keeping the fence line on your L.

The path soon becomes a clear track leading up to East Bexington Farm. Keep the house and barns on the L. At the farm drive, go straight across and stay on the track that skirts round above the barns (waymarked). Enter and leave a small field via the gates, and in the next field go half-R up a slope in the direction of Labour-in-vain farm, in the middle of a group of tall, dark conifers. At the end of this field cross the stile and, keeping the farmhouse with its Lutyensesque outline on the L, go uphill following the R fence line. At the top of the field go straight on over the stile into an area of dense thicket. At the next path junction, go straight on up the slope (fingerpost waymarking: 'Abbotsbury Hill Fort'). This last stretch from the farm up towards the summit of Tulk's Hill is steep. Almost at the top, before reaching the road, turn R following a drystone wall on the R (way-marked: 'Hardy Monument/Osmington Mills'). The

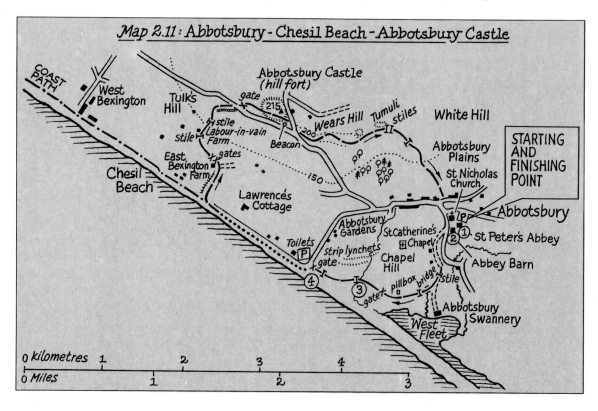

Chesil Beach, The Fleet and Portland Bill.

Iron-Age Abbotsbury hill-fort can be seen ahead. Leave the National Trust's Tulk's Hill Estate via a stile, cross the road and go through the gateway ahead for the hill-fort. Go over the topmost seaward edge of the hill-fort, noticing the fine series of broad and narrow ramparts. At 705 ft (215 m) above sea level, the view from the OS obelisk is superb in all directions.

At the far end of the hill-fort, cross the stile and pass a modern beacon. Cross straight over the lane and continue along the curving ridge of Wear's Hill (waymarked: 'Hardy Monument'). The route passes a series of prehistoric burial cairns.

Cross two stiles in the vicinity of three cairns. Just after the second of these stiles, at the fingerpost, go half-R down the hill (waymarked: 'Abbotsbury'). Go down through an area of hummocks and mini-crags and at the next path junction, by an open-built barn, go through the gate (fingerpost: 'Abbotsbury'). Continue on in the direction of Chapel Hill. Go through another gate and then bear L to pick up and stay on the track that drops down into Abbotsbury.

On reaching the village, go R passing old and new thatched cottages. At the road junction turn L and follow the road back to the car-park.

1   *The church at Abbotsbury*
    Inside St Nicholas Church is an early-Jacobean or late-Tudor pulpit, ornately carved. Two bullet-holes are visible in its canopy. These are said to have been made when the church was attacked during the Civil War by Sir Ashley Cooper, on 8th November, 1644.

Abbotsbury is one of the oldest centres of Christianity in Britain. A church was founded here, dedicated to St Peter, by a priest named Bertulfus before the Abbey was established in the eleventh century. The Abbey was founded by Orc, King Canute's Chief Steward, and it flourished for 500 years before being demolished during the Dissolution.

2 *Abbotsbury tithe barn*
The tithe barn is one of the largest in the country — 270 ft (82.2 m) long and 30 ft (9.1 m) wide. As the Abbey grew in wealth, produce from its holdings was stored here. The Abbey was destroyed by Henry VIII's Commissioners, but the barn and St Catherine's Chapel survived. Nowadays, the barn is used to store locally-grown reed, which is used for thatching roofs in the village. For this reason the barn, unfortunately, is not open to the public.

3 *The Fleet Sanctuary Nature Reserve*
The Fleet Sanctuary Nature Reserve is the second-oldest nature reserve in Great Britain. It dates back to 1393, when official measures were taken to protect its mute swans. The Sanctuary extends over Chesil Beach and includes the entire length of The Fleet lagoon and its landshore margins. The Fleet is of international importance and is a Site of Special Scientific Interest Grade 1*. It is notable for its diversity of waders and wildfowl in winter, which include mallard, teal, pintail, shoveler, pochard, tufted duck, goldeneye and a large population of widgeon. It has the largest, resident mute-swan population in Britain, supported by the Zostera species reed-beds.

It is possible to walk the 8-mile (12.8-km) ridge towards Weymouth between 1 September and 30 April only; i.e., outside the birds' breeding season. This walk can only be done on the lower edge of the seaward side of the ridge, to avoid disturbing wintering waterfowl in The Fleet.

4 *Chesil Beach*
The entire Chesil Beach lies on the Dorset Heritage Coast — part of a national project to protect undeveloped stretches of coastline. It is one of the largest shingle beaches in Britain, stretching for 18 miles (29 km) from the Isle of Portland to West Bay, near Bridport. The pebbles on the ridge are graded in size, with the largest cobbles at the Portland end. Smugglers and fishermen landing on the beach at night were said to be sure of their exact position from the size of the pebbles at a particular spot. The pebbles have derived partly from flint beds in the chalk of the floor of the English Channel, and partly from the varied succession of land-margin rocks.

63

2·12

DEVON

EAST PRAWLE — GAMMON HEAD — PRAWLE POINT — WOODCOMBE POINT

A walk of moderate length which explores Devon's southernmost point, with its rocky cliffs, sheltered coves and wooded combes — all of which combine to make an outstanding area for birds.

ROUTE DESCRIPTION (Map 2.12)

From the village green, with your back to the Pig's Nose public house and the telephone box on your R, go straight on along the road (signposted for pedestrians: 'Prawle Point 1 m'). Follow the road to Ash Park. Here leave the lane and take the public bridlepath track straight ahead (waymarked: 'Public Bridleway Gammon Head 1 m'). Within a short distance the hump of Prawle Point and the jagged outline of Gammon Head come into view and, soon after, the dark outlines of Bolt Tail and Sharp Tor.

At the path junction bear L (yellow waymarking) to drop down towards Gammon Head. At the next path junction, with the east flank of Gammon Head (National Trust) in view, go R to pick up the Coast Path. Here you arrive above the beautiful sandy beach of Maceley Cove *(1)*. Go L along the Coast Path (acorn waymarking). A small steep path (R) drops down to the beach. Continue on the Coast Path around Elender Cove (unfenced). The path skirts Signalhouse Point, and passes above exposed and wave-beaten outcrops of mica schists. A sharp steep climb on the Coast Path is rewarded with views to the south-east over Prawle Point and The Island, and westwards back over Maceley Cove, Gammon Head, Salcombe and Bolt Head.

Go over the stone stile, passing several ancient field boundaries comprising lichen-encrusted flat slabs of mica schist. Continue over Prawle Point passing the coastguard lookout *(2)*. On approaching the row of terraced cottages, go over the stile and continue straight on, keeping the cottages on your L. Just east of the cottages continue straight on the Coast Path via the stile (waymarked 'Lannacombe 2 m'). The National Trust Prawle Point car-park is up on the L.

STARTING AND FINISHING POINT

There are several parking options, hence starting and finishing points; choice will depend on the season and how busy it is. The walk outlined here begins in East Prawle village in a parking area on the edge of the village green (202–781364). A small donation towards the upkeep of the green and churches is requested.

Other parking may be gained by driving past the village green (L) and following the dead-end road almost to its end. Park in the National Trust Prawle Point car-park (L) (202–774355). To join the walk, go down the lane, through the gate and pick up the Coast Path.

RECOMMENDED MAP

OS 1 : 25000 Outdoor Leisure South Devon.

LENGTH

$6\frac{1}{4}$ miles (9.7 km)

ASCENT

One climb: $\frac{3}{4}$ mile (1.2 km) from above Woodcombe Sand towards Woodcombe Farm.

Cross another stile and stay on the Coast Path, which meanders above the present low cliffline. With Lobeater Rock on your L, cross the stone stile and follow the Coast Path around Langerstone Point. Looking back to Prawle Point, you can see a fine natural arch cut into the fractured horneblende schist. With the low relief of Brimpool Rocks on your R cross the stile and skirt round Sharpers Head. Cross another stone stile above Horseley Cove.

Just beyond Horseley Cove the footpath follows the edge of the field round to the L. A path here drops down to the beach – worth the short detour, especially to see birds, including oystercatchers.

Follow the edge of the field to the public right-of-way junction, and here go immediately R (waymarked: 'Coast Path Lannacombe 1 m'). Continue across several small fields and past Maelcombe House. Then go across several more coastal fields and keep with the Coast Path as it follows the low cliff-edge, flanked on the L by the scrub-colonized Woodcombe Point (*3*).

Towards the estuary, Salcombe, from Gammon Head.

After Ballsaddle Rock stay on the Coast Path for a short distance inland, up a valley on the north-east side of Woodcombe Point. At the next footpath junction (before the bungalow) turn L (waymarked 'Public Footpath Woodcombe 1 m'). The return route climbs up through this scrub and field combe via the footpath, which soon becomes a green-lane track. Go through the next gate reached and, with Woodcombe Farm to the R, continue straight on along the track. At the next path junction go through the gate (Public bridleway: 'East Prawle $\frac{1}{2}$ m'). Keep the field hedgebank on the R and follow the edge of the field. On reaching the far end, continue on in the same direction dropping down into a small combe. Go through the gate in the combe, cross the stream and stay on the path to the next junction. Go straight on along the track, soon passing a turning on the L to Maelcombe House. The track becomes a metalled lane leading to East Prawle village.

At the road junction cross straight over and pick up the bridlepath lane by the thatched cottages on the L. On reaching the recent housing development, go through the gate on the R and follow the L field-edge (yellow waymarking). This path weaves its way behind several cottages. On reaching the lane turn L and follow it round to the Pig's Nose public house — so-named after the rock of the same name, which lies just to the north of Gammon Head. The village green is soon reached.

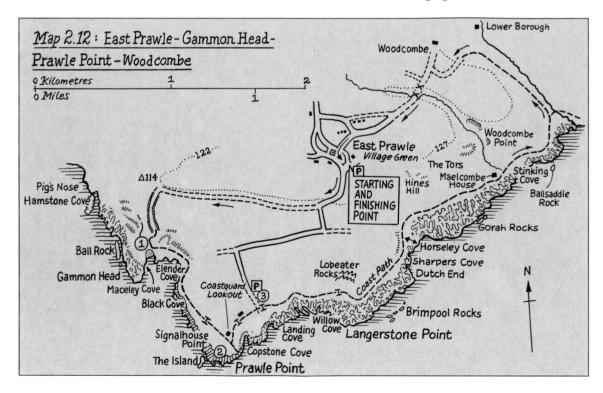

1   *Maceley Cove*

The rocks in this area are some of the oldest in Devon. Some 400 million years ago ancient lava was spewed out, and about 100 million years later these rocks were subjected to intense heat and pressure. As a result, minerals in the rocks were re-arranged into parallel bands. The rocks formed are known as horneblende chlorite schist.

2   *Prawle Point*

Prawle Point is the southernmost tip of Devon and, after the Lizard, forms the second most southerly extremity of mainland Britain.

The word 'Prawle' is derived from the Anglo-Saxon 'prawhyll' or 'prahulle', meaning look-out hill. Many ships have been wrecked and lives lost around the Point. Between the Island and the west side of the Point the 300-ton coaster *Heye-P* was wrecked in 1979.

Prawle Point and area has been designated as a Site of Special Scientific Interest because of its geological and ornithological importance. It is a superb migration watch-point. In winter large numbers of gannets, kittiwakes and auks pass at sea. Turnstones, purple sandpipers and oystercatchers are common. Between December and February there is the possibility of a great northern diver sighting. Spring migrants include manx shearwaters, fulmar, wheat-ears, chiffchaff, goldcrest, firecrest, hobby and the occasional hoopoe (March–May). Late spring sees the arrival of warblers (especially the willow warbler), blackcaps and whitethroats.

Here, too, there is an array of resident birds taking advantage of the immense range of habitats in the area. Cirl bunting is probably more common here than anywhere else in Britain. Buzzards and ravens are often seen overhead, and little owls may be seen perched on rocky outcrops in the daytime.

3   *South Devon Heritage Coast*

South Devon Heritage Coast covers 58 miles (92 km) from Sharkham Point, near Brixham, to Wembury Beach near Plymouth. It was designated, in 1984, by the Countryside Commission because of its outstanding natural beauty, wildlife and historic interest. The South Devon Heritage Coast Service was set up by the South Hams District Council, Devon County Council and the National Trust with grant aid from the Countryside Commission. The Service aims to encourage conservation of the coastal environment, while safeguarding the interests of local people and enabling visitors to enjoy the benefits of the coast.

The route traverses some of the oldest rocks in Devon.

2.13

SOMERSET

CADBURY CASTLE — CORTON DENHAM — SUTTON MONTIS — SOUTH CADBURY

This walk explores south Somerset close to the Dorset border and includes a 1-mile (1.6 km) circuit of Cadbury Castle — the possible site of Arthur's Camelot. The summits of Corton Hill and Corton Ridge are traversed and these offer superb vantage points from which to view the surrounding countryside. The walk also takes in South Cadbury, Corton Denham and Sutton Montis, three unspoilt Somerset villages.

ROUTE DESCRIPTION (Map 2.13)

From the lay-by walk back towards the village and, at the cottage known as Castle Keep (L), take Castle Lane leading to 'Camelot Fort'. Dogs should be kept on a lead. Go through a kissing-gate at the edge of the wood and continue up the track to the topmost rampart. Contour round to the R on the rampart and circuit Cadbury Castle earthworks, a high, flat plateau, from which is a vast panorama down on to the village of Sutton Montis and much of Somerset *(1)*.

Re-trace your way down Castle Lane and turn R on reaching the road (Church Road); continue on, passing the lay-by, for about 440 yards (400 m). At the road junction with Crangs Lane go straight on and within 55 yards (50 m) cross over the wooden stile on the L (waymarked: 'Sigwells 1¼ m'). Cut across the top part of the field to a small footbridge (arrow waymarking). Keep to the L side of this field, and at the end of the field take the grassy track straight ahead (look out for yellow waymarking). Where this track bears L continue straight on along the footpath through the field gate. Keep to the R edge of this field, and at the far end bear R and go in the same direction, keeping the field boundary on the L and walking in the direction of a wooded grove seen in a knoll on Charwell Field. At the far edge of the field, at the track junction, bear R and continue along this enclosed path passing Whitcombe Farm (R). On reaching the road junction, at a grass triangle, turn L and then after 22 yards (20 m) go sharp L up to the top of the minor road. This is a fairly steep ascent that offers

STARTING AND FINISHING POINT

From the A303 dual-carriageway, 2 miles (3.2 km) east of Sparkford take the road to South Cadbury. Drive through the village and park in a lay-by 100 yards (metres) south of Castle Road (183–633253).

LENGTH

7 miles (11 km)

ASCENT

Two short climbs: one approximately ¼ mile (0.4 km) to Cadbury Castle — 164 ft (50 m); the other just over ¼ mile (0.4 km) up the lane leading to The Beacon on Corton Hill — 230 ft (70 m).

good views back to Cadbury Castle and, 12 miles (19.3 km) to the north-west, Glastonbury Tor. At the top of the hill, just past several Scots pine (R), turn sharp R and go through a gate (way-marked: 'Public footpath: Corton Denham 1 m') on to Corton Hill.

Follow the fence line on the L along the crescent-shaped ridge, and then bend to the L to a gate (a small detour can be made for the views from the OS obelisk at some 643 ft/196 m above sea level). Follow the ridge top round above Corton Denham towards the bungalow ahead. On reaching the gate by the bungalow stay in the field and, with your back to this gate, walk down to a small metal gate some 33 yards (30 m) away. On through this gate and keeping Corton Denham church *(2)* on the R, follow the path down the side of Corton Hill to Corton Denham. Cross the

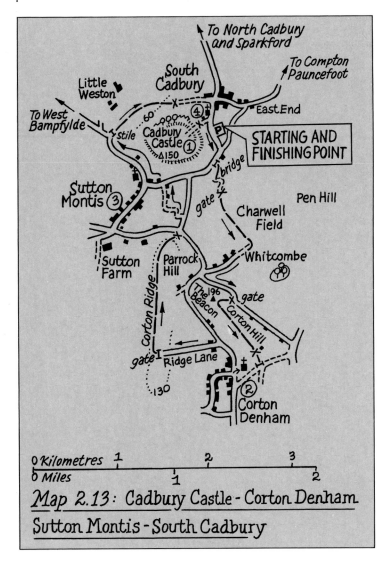

Map 2.13: Cadbury Castle - Corton Denham Sutton Montis - South Cadbury

Sutton Montis huddles beneath the south-west flank of Cadbury Castle.

wooden stile and turn L down the lane, and then R at the road junction. Continue on, passing the Queen's Arms (L) (if you can!). St Andrew's Church is a delight. Go through the village, passing the post office (L). Just beyond the last row of houses turn L down Ridge Lane, passing Yew Tree Farm (L), and follow this up to the summit of Corton Ridge. Go through the gate and turn right. Keeping the field boundary on your R, continue to walk north-west on Corton Ridge.

Continue on the path that skirts around the side of Parrock Hill giving a good view of the southernmost ramparts of Cadbury Castle. Where the path divides, drop down towards the road (a white road sign is just visible). At the bottom of the hill go through the small gate, and along the enclosed green lane to the road. Bear L along the lane and then immediately R (signposted: 'South Cadbury and Compton Pauncefoot') for approximately 100 yards (metres). Turn L on the green lane. On reaching the road at the end of this lane go L and, at the T-junction in Sutton Montis, turn R along the road (signed: 'Little Weston'). Holy Trinity Church should be visited, if only to see the fine Norman chancel arch *(3)*. After the church, follow the lane for about $\frac{1}{2}$ mile (0.8 km) and where it bends to the L take the footpath over the stile on the R (waymarked: 'South Cadbury'). Keep the hedgeline on the L and continue over this pastoral landscape. Go through a gate to follow a track that soon becomes a metalled lane leading back to South Cadbury *(4)*. At the road junction go R up Church Road to return to Cadbury Castle.

1   *Cadbury Castle*
'Truly me seemeth it is a mirakle in bothe arte and nature' and, 'At the very south ende of the chirch of South Cadbyri standith Camallote, sumtyme a famose town or castlelle . . . . The people can telle nothing ther but they had hard say that Arture much resortid to Camalat.'
So wrote John Leland in 1542. Since then, antiquarians and archaeologists have speculated about the claim that Cadbury Castle is the Camelot of Arthurian legend.

Some small excavations took place here in the late nineteenth century and in 1913. In 1965 the Camelot Research Committee was formed, on which Leslie Alcock was Director of Excavations, and attention was centred on Cadbury Castle in 1969 and 1970. It was revealed that the site had been occupied at various times from at least the late Bronze Age, through the Iron Age and into early medieval times. Uncovered in the excavations was a major defensive work, a

Pen Hill from Cadbury Castle.

gateway tower that could be dated to the Arthurian period, and a timber hall. But even today the truth behind the legend remains obscure. The site was strategically placed to defend south-west Britain, and it could well have been the base from which Arthur led troops to the battle of Mons Badonis.

The hill was once thought to be hollow — a fairy refuge where pots of gold were stored. Having fled upon hearing the church bells for the first time, the fairies cast a protective spell so that their treasure sinks deeper into the hill when attempts are made to recover it. Also, King Arthur and his Knights are reputed to sleep in a deep cavern in the hill. Arthur may emerge; watch out for his ghostly rides on Arthur's Hunting Causeway, an old track to Glastonbury.

2 *Corton Denham*

At the time of the Norman Conquest, Corton Denham was known as Corfeton. It obtained the title Denham from Oliver de Dinan, who came from Brittany with William the Conqueror. The first written mention of a parish church here is 1267 but, because of disrepair, it was pulled down in 1869 and re-built in 1870. The new church could also accommodate more people. The architect was Barker-Green. It took 15 months to complete at a cost of £3,400 including the fittings. The church is approached by a small road, or by a cobbled path called 'The Pitchen'. This is believed to have taken its name from the action of those who laid its stones in position.

3 *Sutton Montis church*

Sutton Montis is a parish of more than 1000 years standing. Holy Trinity Church escaped the widespread pulling down of churches in the fourteenth and fifteenth centuries, and its plan and major structure, in consequence, has retained much of its Norman origin (1100–1140). The fine Norman chancel arch is the only one in the area. Also of note are the Early English period chancel windows with their beautiful inner arches. It must be unique that the same family supplied the rectors of the church in unbroken line, by birth or marriage, for 305 years (1573–1878).

4 *South Cadbury church*

The dedication of the church at South Cadbury is to St Thomas à Becket, martyred in Canterbury Cathedral in 1170. The tower, with battlement, pinnacles and a stair turret, dates to the fourteenth century. Like many Somerset churches, the church was totally re-built in the Perpendicular style (1350–1535). The churchyard is well worth a visit. It contains three noble trees — a tulip tree, a yew and a ginkgo. The latter is a particularly beautiful specimen.

2·14

CORNWALL

BODMIN MOOR: ROUGH TOR — BROWN WILLY — LOUDEN HILL

STARTING AND FINISHING
POINT
Large, free car-park (Forestry
Commission/North Cornwall
District Council) 2½ miles
(3.75 km) south-east of Camelford
on Roughtor Road, which leads
off the A39 (highway signing:
'43rd (Wessex) Division War
Memorial'). Roughtor Road is
narrow — drive with care
(200–138818)
MAPS
The walk straddles Landranger
1 : 50 000 Sheets 200 and 201.
Recommended are OS Pathfinder
1 : 25 000 Sheet 1338 — Bodmin
Moor (West), and Sheet SX 08/18
— Camelford.
LENGTH
5 miles (8 km)
ASCENT
Two climbs: ½ mile (0.8 km)
Rough Tor car-park to Showery
Tor 443 ft (135 m); ½ mile
(0.8 km) De Lank River to Brown
Willy 426 ft (130 m)

A walk of moderate length that penetrates the wild fastness of north-west Bodmin Moor. The two highest points in Cornwall are included. This is a dramatic landscape with much of archaeological interest, including one of Cornwall's largest prehistoric stone circles, and deserted prehistoric and medieval settlements. It is not recommended in poor visibility. Dogs must be kept on a lead when visiting Brown Willy.

ROUTE DESCRIPTION (Map 2.14)

From the bottom of the car-park follow the track down and cross the river via the bridge. To the L can be seen the monument to Charlotte Dymond *(1)*. Stay on the track, passing the National Trust's Rough Tor sign.

Walk uphill to Showery Tor — the leftmost outcrop on the ridge. Keep Rough Tor on the R. A distinctive rock pile sits on Showery Tor's summit. A large prehistoric summit cairn is encountered on the tor. From the tor go R, walking along the ridge to Little Rough Tor and Rough Tor. Rough Tor is the second highest point in Cornwall and stands some 1311 ft (400 m) above sea level *(2)*.

From near the southern end of the ridge, cut down the eastern slope of Rough Tor towards Brown Willy. Watch your feet through the clitter. Still heading in the direction of Brown Willy, keep to the L of a clump of trees ahead. Many prehistoric and later field boundaries crisscross these lower slopes. Make for the corner of an intact enclosure wall ahead. Drop down to the De Lank river valley bottom. Go over the river — a tributary of the River Camel — via a low bridge. At the gate is an English Nature sign stating that the land around Brown Willy Tor is privately owned and is a Site of Special Scientific Interest. The landowner kindly allows access to the tor from this point, but the permission does not constitute any legal right of access. A warning is also given that adders are an important component of the natural fauna of the area and should be left alone. Dogs must be

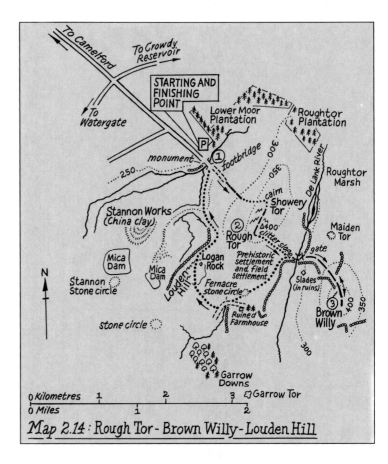

Map 2.14 : Rough Tor - Brown Willy - Louden Hill

Rough Tor.

kept on a lead, and please do not climb walls or fences.

Brown Willy, at 1377 ft (420 m) above sea level, is the highest point in Cornwall. Its name is a corruption of the Cornish 'Bron ewhella' ('the highest hill'). From the summit it is possible to go along the ridge, but do not pass the last rock outcrop. On a clear day the sea is visible to the north and south, and the view takes in much of Bodmin Moor *(3)* and beyond to Dartmoor and Exmoor. The OS obelisk sits on a recent cairn, which in turn sits on a prehistoric round barrow. To the south, halfway along the ridge is a second cairn.

Controlled grazing by sheep, cattle and ponies has maintained the moorland here for centuries. Please avoid disturbing farmstock. Retrace your steps back to the gate by the De Lank River. Recross the bridge and follow the wall (L) back up towards the dramatic outline of Rough Tor. Follow this wall round to the L and keep it close to your L for about 33 yards (30 m). Then strike straight across the open moor, keeping Rough Tor on your R. With Garrow Tor to the quarter-L, make for the Fernacre prehistoric stone circle. From the stone circle, go R to pick up the track seen to the R of a ruined farmhouse. Turn R along the track, cross the stream, and continue on up the track to the point where it begins to level out. From here strike R across the moor to Louden Hill — the Logan Rock is seen to the R of the main outcrop.

From the Logan Rock keep the clay tips to your L and make for the R corner of the stone wall ahead. Strike slightly uphill to avoid marshy ground. Keep Rough Tor on your R and go straight on, for the car-park, over a prehistoric landscape crisscrossed by low boundary works. Here too are prehistoric burial cairns, enclosures and hut circles.

1   *The monument to Charlotte Dymond*
    Charlotte Dymond was murdered in the area on Sunday 4 April, 1844, by her crippled lover, Matthew Weeks. He was hanged for the murder at Bodmin Gaol — an execution witnessed by an alleged 20,000 people.

2   *Rough Tor*
    The remains of a stone fort lie on the summit of Rough Tor, utilizing the granite outcrops of both Little Rough Tor and Rough Tor in its circuit. It is assumed to date from the late Bronze Age, and a dozen round houses can be traced in the south-west part of the interior.

    On top of the tor are the remains of the Chapel of St Michael set in the mutilated remains of a Bronze-Age cairn. The walls are now only just discernible. It was licensed in 1371 and acted as a guide to travellers on the moor. Several

Brown Willy — Cornwall's highest point.

medieval farmsteads existed in the area when the church was in use including Fernacre, Garrow Tor and Louden Hill.

3   *Bodmin Moor*

Bodmin Moor is the largest of the granite uplands of Cornwall, although it is a small, compact area compared to other major British uplands. At the time of the Domesday Book most of the area would have been a continuous tract of moorland. Gilpin, an eighteenth-century traveller to Cornwall, described Bodmin Moor as 'a barren and naked country, in all aspects as uninteresting as can well be conceived'. Today, it is a landscape much altered by forestry, reservoirs, china-clay workings and enclosed grazing, yet it retains considerable wild quality. An extensive enclosing of the moor has taken place in the last 150 years — much was lost in the latter half of the nineteenth century, but some 6671 acres (2700 ha) of moorland has been lost since 1945, 4942 acres (2000 ha) of this since 1960.

2·15

CORNWALL

BODMIN MOOR: MINIONS — THE CHEESEWRING — KILMAR TOR — BEARAH TOR — HENWOOD

A mainly moorland walk that takes in dramatic tor-topped ridges, and many prehistoric and industrial archaeological remains. The route includes a small length ($1\frac{1}{4}$ miles/2 km) of lane walking and some optional tor scrambling. In all, a good introduction to the distinctive quality of Bodmin Moor.

ROUTE DESCRIPTION (Map 2.15)

From the car-parking area, walk up the track for a short distance heading across the open moor. The three prehistoric stone circles known as 'The Hurlers' soon come into view (1). Cut across to the uppermost circle and then bear R (north-east) to reach a gentle ridge within $\frac{1}{2}$ mile (0.8 km) crowned by the prehistoric Rillaton Barrow (2). Walk northwards along the ridge towards Stowe's Hill and the huge naked face of Cheesewring Quarry.

The route crosses many tin surface-workings, and several fenced shafts of the Phoenix mine lodes (veins of metal ore) are encountered on approaching the quarry. Drop down to the R after these shafts and you will come to the trackbed of the former Liskeard and Caradon Railway — the sleeper blocks are well preserved (3). The route passes the granite walls of a ruined gunpowder magazine (L). Walk along the trackbed towards the quarry and then turn L below the spoil heaps. Allow time to explore the area. South-west of the Cheesewring, near the quarry edge, is Daniel Gumb's Cave.

On the west side of the quarry, follow the track northwards for a short distance, and then cut off to the R to walk up to the summit of Stowe's Hill and the balancing rocks of the Cheesewring (4). Two prehistoric stone enclosures encompass Stowe's Hill. The larger of the two, at the northern end of the hill, contains a large number of hut foundations. Head north over the summit; to the L on Craddock Moor you can see the Gold-Digging Quarry and its spoil heaps. This was last worked in the 1930s. Drop down the north side of the hill. The hamlet of Sharptor is seen to the R and to the L is Wardbrook Farm.

STARTING AND FINISHING POINT
Small car-park at the south-west end of Minions village (St Cleer road). Look out for English Heritage sign 'The Hurlers'. $2\frac{3}{4}$ miles (4.5 km) north of Liskeard (201–259711).
LENGTH
$6\frac{1}{2}$ miles (10.5 km)
ASCENT
Three climbs: $\frac{1}{2}$ mile (0.8 km) from the Hurlers to Rillaton Barrow — 98 ft (30 m); 250 m up the west flank of Stowe's Hill — 98 ft (30 m). Option: $\frac{3}{4}$ mile (1.2 km) from Bearah Tor quarry to Sharp Tor — 197 ft (60 m).

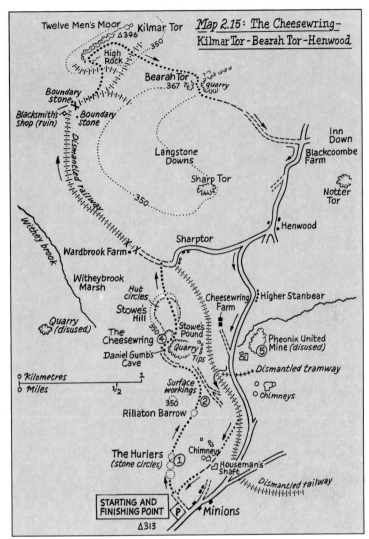

On reaching the farm track turn L, and at the farm go through the gate on the R of the farmhouse. Continue straight on along the track, passing through a gateway. Across these enclosures, gates should be shut and dogs kept under close control. At the next gateway continue straight on, ignoring the track leading up hill on the R. Stay on the track — the trackbed of the Kilmar Railway, built in 1858 to serve granite workings at Kilmar Tor. The track passes through a large enclosure with the broad sweep of the Withey Brook on the L. After the next gate keep on the track, Newel Tor and a large prehistoric field system and settlement can be seen on the L. Smallacoombe Plantations dominate the hill beyond. The mineral railway track soon curves round to

The Hurlers, with the engine-house of a nineteenth-century mine beyond.

the R to give a full view of the dramatic rock ridge of Kilmar Tor. On approaching the gate that leads onto the open moor on the L are the remains of a blacksmith's shop once associated with the granite workings in the area. Go through the gate and continue straight on, passing a Rillaton Manor boundary stone on the L (on the R can be seen another boundary stone on the skyline).

On reaching the second stone-built loading ramp on the L side of the railway go L for the west flank of the tor-topped ridge (High Rock). The route crosses a branch line of the railway. To avoid tor scrambling, walk on the southern flank of the tor. About one-third along the ridge go half-R in the direction of Bearah Tor, which is flanked to the R by Sharp Tor. Cross the trackbed of the railway once more.

Continue across the wild open moor for the mid-point of Bearah Tor Ridge (1204 ft/367 m above sea level). Go over to the south side of the tor and bear L for Bearah Tor Quarry.

Follow the track down, go through a gate and reach the lane. Here, at Blackcoombe Farm, go R. A short ascent along the tree-lined lane is followed by a descent into the village of Henwood. At the road junction turn R, and at the next junction, by the telephone box, go R (highway signed: 'Sharptor/Minions'). Stay on this lane uphill and then pass the dead-end road leading off R to Sharptor. Proceed along the lane, looking back now and again for excellent views of Sharp Tor. Pass the hamlet of Higher Stanbear (L) and Phoenix United Mine comes into view *(5)*.

Just beyond where the Cheesewring Farm track meets the lane (R) cut R uphill to pick up a dismantled, inclined tramway. On reaching the track go L. At the next track junction continue straight on, ignoring the track leading off on the L, which drops down to a small group of houses.

An engine-house soon comes into view on the R. Here, leave the track and pass this engine-house. This was built at Houseman's Shaft of the South Phoenix Mine in 1853. Just beyond the ruin strike across the moor (R), heading in the direction of another distant engine-house — the Silver Valley Mine on Craddock Moor. The Hurlers stone circles are soon reached. Strike half-L for the return to the car-park.

1   The Hurlers

The Hurlers, now in the care of English Heritage, are three partly restored Bronze-Age stone circles aligned roughly north-east to south-west. The stones, many of which have been re-erected, are between 2 and 6 ft (0.6 and 2.0 m) tall. In the late sixteenth century, locals believed the stones had once been men, transformed for profaning the Lord's Day with hurling the ball — a once widespread Cornish pastime.

2   *Rillaton Barrow*

Rillaton round barrow also dates to the Bronze Age. It is 120 ft (37 m) in diameter and 8 ft (2.4 m) high. On its east side is a stone cist. The centre of the barrow has been robbed by a deep excavation. Nineteenth-century excavations yielded a skeleton accompanied by a bronze dagger and the famous Rillaton cup. The latter is a ribbed cup of beaten gold similar in style to gold and silver vessels from Mycenae. The cup was lost for a number of years, but was rediscovered in King George v's dressing-room. The cup is now in the British Museum.

3   *The Liskeard and Caradon Railway*

The construction of the Liskeard and Caradon Railway in 1844 facilitated the development of the Cheesewring Quarry. Deepening of the quarry in the early 1870s saw a new branch line at a lower level to serve the export of granite off the moor for a growing market. The fine silver-grey granite was highly sought for engineering and architectural work, including Devonport Dockyard, the Thames embankment, Westminster and Tower Bridges, and breakwaters at Alderney and Dover. At its peak, over 100 people were employed here.

Encircling the main summit rocks are fleur-de-lis marks cut into the rock. These, with other markings, were cut in the nineteenth century to define protective limits. The protection of the Cheesewring outcrop resulted in only a small amount of work being carried out after World War I.

4   *Cheesewring*

The dramatic Cheesewring stands over 20 ft (6.1 m) high. In 1796, denouncing the feature being attributed to the Druids, Dr Maton commented that it was 'probably constructed by nature herself, in one of her whimsical moments'. It is a famous landmark wherein, as John Norden put it, 'Nature hath done more at adventure than arte or force can doe by greatest deliberation'.

By 1869 the quarry face had encroached so close to the Cheesewring that supporting stones were erected on one side of the outcrop in case it should be shaken and topple during blasting operations.

5   *The Phoenix United Mine*

The Phoenix United Mine was once the largest tin producer in east Cornwall. The main period of operation was between 1842 and 1898, when the mine yielded considerable quantities of tin and copper. The engine-house and associated buildings date from 1907–14, when an unsuccessful attempt was made to re-open the mine.

The Cheesewring — a distinctive granite outcrop.

81

2·16

CORNWALL

THE LIZARD: KYNANCE COVE − GRADE − CADGWITH − OLD LIZARD HEAD

STARTING AND FINISHING POINT

Follow the A3083 Helston-Lizard road to approximately 1 mile (1.6 km) north of Lizard village. Here go R (signed: 'Kynance Cove: National Trust'). Drive with care along this lane ('sleeping policemen' ramps) to the large car-park on the L (203–688134). A toll in the main visiting season will have to be paid, otherwise voluntary contributions welcomed.

LENGTH

8 miles (12.75 km)

ASCENT

Level walking inland route except climb out of Kynance Cove − 197 ft (60 m). Several short, coastal climbs.

This walk explores the superb and distinct 'heel' of Cornwall − Land's End being the 'toe'. An inland route over the Lizard Downs to Cadgwith enables a return route via the Coast Path skirting round the most southerly tip of mainland Britain. Exploration of Kynance Cove is best made at low tide. In the height of the visitor season, while much of the coastline is remote, some areas can be very busy; patience, tolerance, or avoidance are recommended! See also OS Pathfinder Series (1–25 000) 1372.

ROUTE DESCRIPTION (Map 2.16)

From the National Trust car-park take the seaward path that leads to the view point − 200 ft (61 m) above the sea overlooking Kynance Cove, Asparagus Island, Gull Rock, Lion Rock, and south to Old Lizard Head (Lizard Point). Retrace your steps to the car-park and go L following the newly-made-up paths down to the cove (waymarked). Tide and time permitting, the cove, its sand and fragmented pieces of land should be explored (1).

From the cove, follow the track leading up the valley (the Ky-nans or 'Dog's Brook'). At the point where this track levels out, strike L along the broad, well-trodden bridlepath over the Lizard plateau. Ignore the next waymarked footpath on the L and continue straight over Lizard Downs, staying on the bridlepath, which can be muddy in places. To the L on the skyline can be seen the remains of a windmill. This seemingly uninteresting piece of level heathland contains much of ecological significance (2). The bridlepath meets the A3083 Helston-Lizard road to the L of a row of houses. This last stretch can be very muddy.

Cross straight over the road to go along the track ahead (to the L of the houses). This track soon becomes a path passing through a scrubby thicket and then it opens out on to a small area of heath with views over to the serpentine and granite tower of St Grade's Church (St Grada of the Holy Cross). The path then enters another area of thicket, and this rutted section can also be muddy. On reaching the road go R.

82

At the next road junction continue straight on along the lane towards Grade. Within a short distance turn on to the footpath on the L (waymarked) to the church, which stands in conspicuous isolation.

Leave the churchyard at its eastern end via a stone stile. Keeping the field hedge on your L go straight on to the bottom of the field. Then follow the short stretch of enclosed path that leads into another field. Keeping near to the edge of this field brings you to the lane ahead at Prazegooth. Cross the road and continue down the lane, keeping Metheven House on the R. Here go L along the metalled track (waymarked: 'Public footpath to Cadgwith'), which soon becomes unmetalled.

On reaching the metalled lane that drops down to the unspoilt fishing village of Cadgwith, go R along the Coast Path (waymarked: 'Devil's Frying Pan').

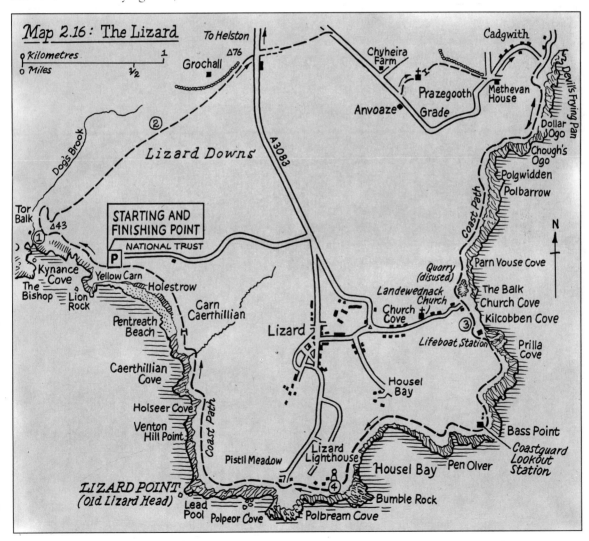

The Coast Path leads up through a well-maintained garden. Near the top of the hill go L (acorn waymarking: 'Coast Path') passing Town Place — a small cottage on the R. The return route to Kynance Cove hugs the coastline by way of the Coast Path. The Coast Path (unfenced) skirts high above the Devil's Frying Pan (National Trust) — a great hole in which the tide surges in through a cave below.

A small quarry is passed above Chough's Ogo, and the route then continues on the cliff-top over Polgwidden, with good views to Bass Point and the Lifeboat Station at Kilcobben Cove. Dropping down to Church Cove, the route passes more quarries. These serpentine quarries provided stone for the runways at Culdrose airfields. Crushed serpentine was also used for firebricks. Inland can be seen Landewednack Church — the most southerly church in Britain. The church is dedicated to St Wynwallo, a Celt who founded the famous Abbey of Landevennec in Brittany.

The Coast Path brings you to Kilcobben Cove. It is here that the Lifeboat is situated, replacing both the one at Lizard Point (Polpeor Cove) and the one at Cadgwith (3). From Kilcobben Cove the next headland is Bass Point. The route passes in front of the Coastguard Lookout Station and then to the headland of Pen Olver. On its eastern side is a deep inlet. The Lizard lighthouse soon comes into view and Bumble Rock protrudes from the water like a huge shark's tail-fin.

Continue on past the Housel Bay Hotel (refreshments available) and drop down into Housel Cove. The hotel here has seen eminent guests, including Prince George (later King George V) and C. L. Dodgson (Lewis Carroll). A short climb out of the Cove brings you near to Lizard lighthouse. The Lion's Den, or Daws Ogo is another great hole formed by a collapsed cave — the collapse took place on the night of 19 February, 1847.

Pass the Lizard Lighthouse (4) and continue on to England's most southerly tip. A variety of succulent plants grow in profusion here, including Hottentot figs and smaller mesembryanthemums. On reaching the car-park drop down to Polpeor Cove, the site of the original slipway for the Lizard lifeboat. Retrace your steps to the car-park (cafés open in season) and pass the monumental plaque depicting the 'Record of the Services and Boat Records of the Lizard Lifeboats of the Royal National Lifeboat Institute'.

Continue on the Coast Path in a west-north-west direction, to come to Pistil (Pistol) Meadow (National Trust).

From Old Lizard Head (Lizard Down) there are superb views along the coastline to Pentreath Beach, Kynance Cove and Rill Point. The Coast Path skirts high above Holseer Cove and drops

Opposite: Gull Rock, Kynance Cove.

into and climbs out of Caerthillian Cove, where the sea relentlessly pounds the cliffs. The Coast Path leaves the cliff edge, via a stile, and enters a field to avoid a dangerous section of cliff ahead. It then continues over Holestrow and Yellow Carn, from which is a fine view southwards back over Pentreath Beach and Old Lizard Head. From here it is only a short walk back to the car-park.

1   *Kynance Cove*

Francis Kilvert visited Kynance Cove in 1870 and recorded in his diary that he 'never saw anything like the wonderful colour of the serpentine rocks, rich, deep, warm, variegated, mottled and streaked and veined with red, green and white, huge blocks and masses of precious stone . . . on every side, an enchanted cove'. The cove is an inspiring place and holds many named, distinctive coastal features: Asparagus Island, Mulvan, Tailor, Man-o'-War, Steeple Rock, The Parlour, The Devil's Letterbox, The Devil's Bellows, The Drawing-Room and Devil's Mouth.

The Devil's Bellows is a narrow fissure from which is sent an occasional violent water spout with accompanying thundering rumbles. The Devil's Post Office is another opening in the rock; Victorian travellers were encouraged to hold a letter over its mouth, where the indraught of air would snatch it from their hands and carry it to a mysterious receiver below. The caves and other features in the cove can be explored, but care must be given to the state of the tide.

2   *The Lizard*

The cliffs and heaths in the Lizard area form one of the classical botanical areas in the British Isles. Unusual soil formations and geographical position and aspect combine to make much of the flora, the best representation of 'Lusitanian' species and other local rarities. The underlying rocks are also of considerable importance and great complexity, and include serpentine, granite, and gneiss and horneblende schists.

An interesting heather species growing on the Lizard is the Cornish Heath (*Erica vagans*), which is not known to grow naturally elsewhere in Britain except for one or two very restricted sites. Butterflies to be seen on the heath in summer include small and large skippers, small copper, common blue, grayling, meadow brown and small heath, and the rare sighting of the occasional arrival of a migrant milkweed — or Monarch — butterfly may be had. Cuckoos, corn bunting, lapwing, grasshopper warblers, meadow pipits, skylarks, wheatears and stonechats breed on the heaths. There is also an abundance of birds of prey; watch out for buzzard, hen harrier, Montagu's harrier, hobby, merlin and sparrowhawk.

3 *Lizard Lifeboat station*

Nowhere in Britain were there three lifeboat stations on a 6-mile (9.6-km) stretch of coast, as there once were at Coverack, Cadgwith and The Lizard. At Kilcobben Cove the lifeboat has replaced both the one at Lizard Point (Polpeor Cove) and the one at Cadgwith. The former slipway at Polpeor Cove faced the full force of south-westerly gales, while Kilcobben offers a degree of protection. The new station was opened by the Duke of Cornwall in 1961 and is now known as the Lizard Lifeboat Station. The Tyne Class lifeboat has a top speed of 18 knots and a crew of six.

On the night of 17 March, 1907, and throughout the next day, four Lizard peninsula lifeboats took part in the greatest-ever rescue operation undertaken by RNLI lifeboats. The White Star Liner, *Suevic*, got stranded on the Maeheere Reef in thick fog and heavy seas. All 524 persons on board were rescued without loss.

4 *The Lizard Lighthouse*

The Lizard coastline, before the days of radar, was a graveyard to many vessels. However, in the sixteenth century an initial proposal to establish a light was violently opposed by locals. The official objection was that it could be used as a navigation aid for pirates and unfriendly powers. However, another reason was the substantial gains to be reaped from shipwrecks.

In the early seventeenth century Sir John Killigrew achieved Royal consent for a light. His main motive was to gain revenue by charging dues to any vessel that sailed by in safety. A light burned at a cost of 10 shillings (50p) a night for coal. Opposition persisted and dues were difficult to collect. Eventually the project was abandoned.

In 1752 another light, a double coal-burning structure, was established. In about 1790 Trinity House took responsibility for the light, and replaced it with the present twin towers. These lights were converted from coal to oil in 1812. In 1878 an improved foghorn was positioned, replacing an earlier crude fog signal. In 1903 the Lizard became a single light, and the adoption of electricity made it the most powerful light in the British Isles, being visible out to sea for more than 20 miles (32 km). The lighthouse is open to visitors between Easter and October, but not on foggy days or, at the time of writing, on Sundays.

Polbream Cove and the Lizard lighthouse.

2·17

CORNWALL

WEST PENWITH: ZENNOR — WICCA — TROWAN — HELLESVEOR CLIFF — ZENNOR HEAD

STARTING AND FINISHING
POINT
Small car-park in Zennor village,
which can be busy in the peak
holiday season (203–454383). It
is 4¼ miles (7 km) west of St Ives,
just off the B3306.
MAP
OS Pathfinder 1 : 25 000 Series
Sheet 33/43.
LENGTH
8½ miles (13.6 km)
ASCENT
Several short coastal climbs.

This walk explores a superb granite landscape, and all of the route is in the West Penwith Environmentally Sensitive Area. The inland route crosses a distinctive landscape of small fields by way of the Zennor church path (the Tinners' Way), which links farm with farm. The return is by way of the South West Coast Path — rough going in places along a spectacular coastline.

ROUTE DESCRIPTION (Map 2.17)

Go up the lane to the church *(1)*. From the church, go over the Cornish-style cattle grid on the north-west corner of the church-yard. These distinctive 'stiles' consist of slabs of granite. The one here was placed at an entrance to the churchyard to prevent cattle from entering. Turn immediately R up the track. Follow the L-hand field boundary wall crossing a stone stile.

The route, an old church path now labelled the Tinners' Way, then crosses a unique landscape of small fields via a series of grids and stiles in the walls. Keep on roughly the same line for the farmstead of Tremedda. At Tremedda, cross the lane and continue straight on over the next stone grid. Follow the electricity line for the route across the next field to Tregerthen. Keep to the R of the farm and from here go on in the same direction along an enclosed path, still following the line of electricity poles. Black and white marker posts soon denote the position of most of the grids and stiles encountered.

At Wicca go through the farmyard and continue straight on along the farm track to Boscubben. Just past Boscubben farmhouse the track divides. Take the L fork down for about 40 yards (35 m) and then go R over the stone stile with a marker post by it. The path now leads to Trendrine. Keep to the L of the farm and here you will see a Tinners' Way marker post — one of a series bearing a black motif. From Trendrine head for Trevassa Farm *(2)*. From here turn L on to the lane and then go immediately R by Little Trevega. The electricity line then helps to mark the next stretch across to a lane. Go over the stile here and turn R. After about 195 yards (180 m) go L following the Tinners' Way signs. The next farm is Trevalgan. The route passes to the L of the farm. Keep on a straight line ahead for the next farmstead — Trowan. From here a clearly marked path, in the same direction across more fields, brings you to a farm track. Here, at this footpath crossroads, go L to join the South West Coast Path at Hellesveor Cliff.

Go L (westwards) along the Coast Path. From Pen Enys Point headland is a superb view back along the coast. Trevega Cliff reaches 300 ft (91 m) above sea level and offers a good view to the west. Pass River Cove and off-shore you can see the group of rocks known as The Carracks — a good place for grey seals. The Coast Path skirts high above Wicca Pool — a superb sea-smashed inlet. Between Wicca and Tregerthen Cliffs a small

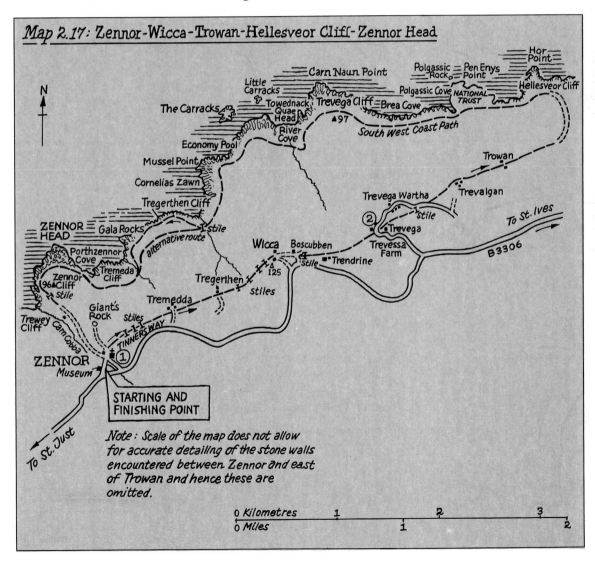

Map 2.17: Zennor-Wicca-Trowan-Hellesveor Cliff-Zennor Head

Note: Scale of the map does not allow for accurate detailing of the stone walls encountered between Zennor and east of Trowan and hence these are omitted.

Bench end, the Mermaid Chair, Zennor church.

stream plunges down to the sea. Cross this stream and go over the stile. Here you can turn R along the lower coast path, which will involve some rough scrambling in places. The not-so-adventurous should continue straight on from the stile over Tregerthen Cliff.

On approaching Zennor Cliff take the lower (R) path, which skirts above and around Porthzennor Cove and Zennor Head (Coast Path waymarking). Once around Zennor Head, leave the Coast Path via the stone stile. Pass Carn Cobba (Coastguard) on the R and follow the lane back to Zennor.

1   Zennor church

Undoubtedly there was a small Celtic church on the site, probably from the 6th century AD. The present twelfth-century church is dedicated to St Senara, the patron saint of Zennor. One of the windows in the south side of the chancel depicts her holding the church. An additional aisle was added in 1451 on the north side of the church. In 1890 the church was in a sad state of neglect but was subsequently carefully restored.

In the side chapel stands the Mermaid Chair. The date of the carving is uncertain but it may be 500 to 600 years old. According to legend, a beautiful young woman in a long dress used to sit at the back of the church seemingly entranced by the singing of a chorister named Matthew Trewhella. One evening she lured him down into the sea at Pendour (Mermaid's) Cove. If you listen carefully on warm summer evenings you may hear the pair of lovers singing together. In the Middle Ages the symbol of a mermaid was used to teach people about the human and divine natures of Christ.

2   West Penwith

Much of north-west Penwith has been designated as an Environmentally Sensitive Area (ESA) by the Ministry of Agriculture. ESAs have been selected for their landscape, historic and wildlife value and where traditional farming methods would help to maintain this value. West Penwith has been farmed for about 5000 years and it is noted for its granite-walled homesteads and the intricate arrangement of stone-hedged fields.

Opposite: Zennor Head.

CORNWALL

West Penwith: Carn Galver — Mên-an-tol — Chûn Downs — Morvah — Bosigran Castle

STARTING AND FINISHING POINT
Small National Trust car-park on the north side of the St Just/St Ives road (B3306) at Carn Galver Mine, $1\frac{3}{4}$ miles (2.8 km) east of Morvah, 3 miles (5 km) south-west of Zennor (203–362424).
MAP
OS Pathfinder 1 : 25 000 Sheet 1364.
LENGTH
$8\frac{3}{4}$ miles (14 km)
ASCENT
Several short coastal climbs, and $\frac{3}{4}$ mile (1.2 km) over the col south of Carn Galver — 410 ft (125 m); $\frac{1}{2}$ mile (0.4 km) from Trehyllys farm to Chûn Castle — 164 ft (50 m)

This superb walk traverses wild moors — home to buzzard, ravens, kestrels, skylarks, linnets, legends and myths. It includes some of the best of Cornwall's archaeology, including prehistoric chamber tombs and hill-forts and the mysterious Mên-an-tol, as well as encountering evidence of the area's tin-mining past. The walk ends along some of the most rugged coastline on the south-west peninsula, and includes the spectacular site of the Iron-Age Bosigran Castle. Some lane walking.

Route Description (Map 3.18)

From the car-park, dominated by the restored pumping and whim engine-houses of Carn Galver Mine, turn R down the road. Just beyond the highway 'Road narrows' sign, take the track on the L leading up over White Downs col with the tor-topped ridge of Carn Galver (Goats Carn) on the L and Watch Croft on the R.

Over the hill, the route now follows an ancient trackway in the direction of the engine-houses of Ding Dong Mine on the far horizon. Hannibal's Carn and Little Galver are seen to the L. At the Four Parishes Stone is a track crossroads. Turn L here and follow the path if you wish to visit the Boskednan Stone circle, also known as 'The Nine Maidens' ($\frac{3}{4}$ mile/1.2 km there and back).

Standing at the track crossroads, with the prominent engine-house of the Ding Dong Mines on your L, you can see the solitary upright stone of the Mên Scryfa ahead in a field. Walk along the track in the direction of this stone. Just past a farm ruin on the R, the track divides — take the L fork (yellow waymarking) along the hedged track. Access to the Mên Scryfa stone is gained by a stone stile from the track at the far end of the field *(1)*. Retrace your steps to the track and continue straight on to the signpost (L) to the Mên-an-tol, or 'holed stone' *(2)*. Turn L over the stile here and continue on the path leading to this famous and mysterious monument.

From the far end stone, follow the path that strikes off through the gorse in the direction of the Ding Dong Mine engine-house. The path is a little prickly at first, and crosses a small stream. After crossing this stream stay on the path bearing half-L. Again the path becomes prickly in places. It then crosses a low boundary wall with the engine-house directly ahead.

From the engine-house *(3)*, which sits on the Greenburrow shaft, there are extensive views over the moors of West Penwith. From here go R, over the wall, and follow the well-trodden footpath down, passing mining tips and pits. Stay on this track and, at the point where it meets a boundary wall on the R, to the L several fields away can be seen Lanyon Quoit. Keep this boundary wall on your R until reaching a metal gate. Here, go over a crude stone stile (yellow waymarking) and follow the enclosed track to the road. Turn L up the road to visit Lanyon Quoit, a prehistoric Chamber Tomb (a $\frac{1}{2}$ mile/0.8 km there and back detour) *(4)*. Retrace your steps down the road passing Lanyon Farm and cross the valley bottom. Ignore the next road junction on the L (from which an otherwise convenient green lane has unfortunately been blocked off). At the next road junction, at the telephone box, near the Mên-an-tol studio and print workshop, turn L. Continue on this lane uphill and then pass Kerrow Farm entrance (R). Where the lane swings round sharp L, go straight on (signed 'Trehyllys Farm and Chûn Castle and Quoit'). On reaching the farm, keep the farmhouse on the R and turn uphill R for Chûn Castle (waymarked a little distance uphill) *(5)*.

From the Iron Age hill-fort of Chûn Castle go L for Chûn Quoit. From Chûn Quoit, retrace your steps in the direction of Chûn Castle for about 16 yards (15 m) and go L along the path through the heath, keeping the field boundary on the L. As the path drops down to Chûn, Crofto and Carne farms, there is a fine view over numerous small enclosures and the hamlet of Morvah. The path soon becomes enclosed by two drystone walls for a short distance and then meets the track to Chûn. Here, go L and at the next junction go R towards Crofto. Ignore the next turning to Hendra and Crofto. Leave the track on the L at the bend on approaching Carne Farm via the stone stile (waymarked 'Permissive path — not dedicated as a highway'). This path then cuts across the field to another stone stile to the R of field clearance stones up against the stone wall (yellow waymarking). Go through the next field and continue on in the same direction through several fields, via the stone stiles, with Morvah church ahead (yellow waymarking).

At the road go L and then first R at Morvah. On the L just before the church stands a rusting Gilbarro petrol pump outside a former Board School (1882), now a barn. From the churchyard

Rural change, Morvah

The Mên-an-tol.

go L and then over the stone stile (L). Keeping the churchyard wall on the L continue on the sunken path. Go through the next gateway and stay on this path, which offers a good view back over to the church. Go over a crude stile at the end of the path and drop down to the Coast Path, keeping a small building on your L. Turn R on to the Coast Path and ahead lies a stretch of superb coast scenery with Bosigran Cliff and the rocky headland of Gurnard's Head now in view.

The return route to Carn Galver Mine is by way of this rugged section of the Coast Path. You soon pass a ruined mine on the L — notice the turfed over buddles where tin ore was separated. The cliff-top continues over Rosemergy, where huge castellated granite crags drop to the sea. Continuing on the Coast Path, the walk soon ends with Carn Galver Mine in view as well as the sheer wall of Bosigran Cliff towering above Porthmoina Cove, a seething, wild place.

Stay on the Coast Path, crossing a small stream just above a ruined building on the L. Continue up on to Bosigran Castle — this Iron-Age cliff castle stands on one of the West Penwith peninsula's highest and most spectacular headlands. Take care on the headland as many paths end at the top of sheer rock faces.

Retrace your steps down to the path junction and head inland on the path towards the engine-houses for the return to the car-park. The isolated cottage on the L at Bosigran belongs to the Climbers' Club of Great Britain.

1   *The Mên Scryfa stone*
The Mên Scryfa inscribed stone, some 6 ft (1.8 m) tall, dates to the sixth century AD. On its northern face is an inscription to RIALOBRAN — CVNOVAL — FIL (Rialobran, son of Cunoval), their names meaning respectively 'Royal Raven' and 'Famous Chieftain'. The stone may have been a Bronze-Age menhir before being put to Christian use, and some believe it to mark the grave of the Royal Raven who was allegedly killed on this spot in a battle.

2   *The Mên-an-tol stone*
The Mên-an-tol is assumed to be Bronze Age, but is of unknown purpose. The wheel-shaped slab, 4 ft 3 in (1.3 m) across, is set on edge and pierced by a large, round hole. It is flanked by two small upright stones 4 ft (1.2 m) high and there is a third recumbent stone. The stones are thought to have originally stood in a triangle. Also known as the 'Crick Stone', the monument is attributed with healing and prophetic powers. Naked children were passed three times through the hole and drawn along the grass three times in an easterly direction — a cure for scrofula (a form of tuber-

culosis) and rickets. Adults sought relief from rheumatism, spine troubles or ague by crawling through the hole nine times against the sun. Two brass pins were placed on top of the stone and their movements used for augury. Fertility rites have also been interpreted from its female and male connotations.

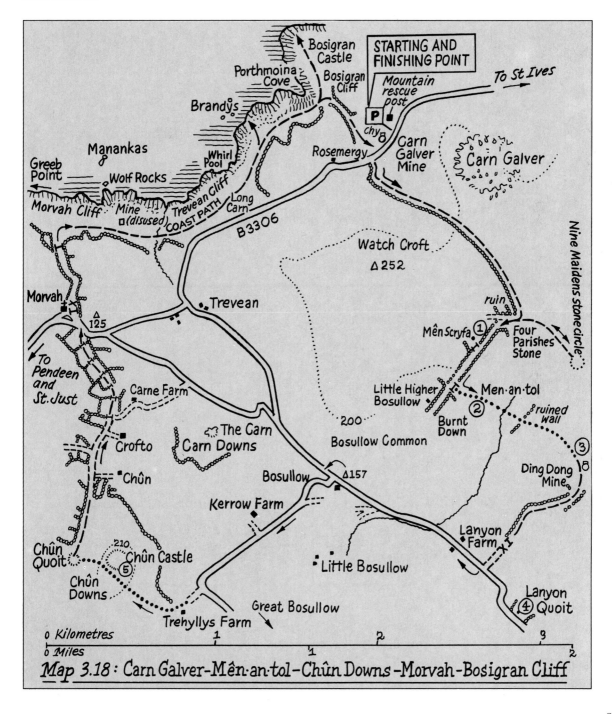

Map 3.18: Carn Galver–Mên·an·tol–Chûn Downs–Morvah–Bosigran Cliff

Opposite: Chûn Quoit.

3   *Ding Dong Mine*

Ding Dong Mine engine-house is situated high on the moorlands. At one time the mine possessed a windmill that was used to pump water from the workings. In about 1857 some 200 miners were employed here, nearly a third were boys under 15 years of age. In common with other Cornish mines, local girls were also employed. These women and young girls used hammers to break and separate the ore from waste rock. The Ding Dong Bell, swung to signal the start and finish of the working shifts at the mine, is now kept in the church at Madron. The mine closed in 1878 with over 10 miles (16 km) of levels below ground. The area abounds in unfenced shafts — care must be taken.

4   *Lanyon Quoit*

Lanyon Quoit Neolithic tomb, dating possibly to 2000 BC, bears very little resemblance to its original form. It has lost its covering mound, and during a storm in 1815 it fell and some stones were broken. True construction could not be achieved when it was re-erected in 1824 after public subscription. A man on horseback can no longer pass beneath the huge capstone as he could when William Borlase visited the site in 1769. A legend claims that a giant's bones were found in it — the monument is also known as 'Giant's Quoit' or 'Giant's Table'. The monument was given to the National Trust in 1952.

5   *Chûn Castle*

Chûn Castle is a superb Iron-Age hill-fort, with a diameter of 93 yards (85 m) built entirely from stone. It comprises two massive concentric walls, the heights of which have been reduced by stone robbing. Within the fort is a stone-lined well and the foundations of Dark-Age buildings dating to the sixth century AD which were built against the back of the inner wall. These overlay the sites of at least a dozen Iron-Age round houses — pottery found here dates to the third and second centuries BC. Just south of the well, excavations revealed a smelting furnace and lumps of tin slag. The fortress entrance was probably altered to its present ingenious staggered design by its re-occupants.

3·19

SOMERSET

SOMERSET LEVELS — KING'S SEDGEMOOR DRAIN AND RIVER CARY — BAWDRIP — SOMERTON

STARTING AND FINISHING POINT
Bawdrip village. Park with consideration in the wide street near the church (182–342395). Bawdrip lies just to the south of the A39, 1 mile (1.5 km) south-east of Puriton, $9\frac{1}{2}$ miles (15.2 km) west of Street.
FINISHING POINT
Somerton market square (193–490285)
MAP
The walk is covered mainly by OS Landranger 182, but the last $1\frac{1}{2}$ miles (2.4 km) to Somerton falls on Sheet 193.
LENGTH
$13\frac{1}{2}$ miles (21.7 km)
ASCENT
Level walking with one short gradual climb up to Somerton.

The cutting of the King's Sedgemoor Drain in the late eighteenth century caused a single dramatic change in the landscape — the re-routing of a whole river. The walk over a flat landscape follows the Drain side for some $7\frac{1}{2}$ miles (12 km) — crossing over a great number of stiles on route — and continues along the River Cary to the ancient town of Somerton. After rain the paths may be muddy; after heavy or persistent rain flooding may occur in the area, making the walk impossible.

ROUTE DESCRIPTION (Map 3.19)

From the porch of St Michael and All Angels church, in the centre of Bawdrip village, cross over the churchyard and at the lane turn R, passing the primary school. Within 15 yards (metres), at the road junction, go L down Bradney Lane. Cross Bradney Bridge over King's Sedgemoor Drain and at the National Rivers Authority Bradney Depot, turn immediately L along the footpath. Pass Bradney Pumping Station (L) and follow the footpath, keeping the Drain on the L. A whole succession of stiles are crossed en route. The view is flanked on the L by the wooded slopes of Pendon Hill, and the low-lying West Moor *(1)*.

On reaching the lane at Parchey Bridge, go through the gate and the gate opposite. Follow the path round a side channel of the Drain, go over the stile and continue on the next stretch of the Drain with some 23 stiles to cross. Pendon Hill gives way to the low ridge of Ball Hill and Pit Hill (L), and to the R is seen the tall tower of Weston Zoyland church. Just after the row of pylons the Drain bends markedly to the L; look across to the R over Lang Moor — this was the site of the Battle of Sedgemoor, 6 July 1685 — the last battle to be fought on English soil.

Continue along the Drain to the next footbridge. It is worth crossing to the mid-point of this bridge for remarkable views up- and downstream *(2)*.

Recross the bridge to continue with the Drain still on your L. More stiles await on the next stretch to Greylake Bridge. Langacre Rhyne is crossed en route via a footbridge, and here there are good views to Middlezoy church. This section of the landscape is sub-divided by barbed wire fencing — some stiles are in poor condition but negotiable.

On approaching Greylake Bridge, keep the field barbed-wire fence on the L; the small rhyne before the bridge requires negotiating as well as barbed wire and wind-blown willows. Pass the disabled and elderly anglers' provision and go through the gate to the road. Cross the road and go through the gate opposite — medieval engineers made the Greylake Fosse across King's Sedge Moor as a causeway.

Follow the Drain-side path, passing through three gates. Aller Wood and Breach Wood are seen to the R. Yet more stiles/fence lines are crossed as you continue over King's Sedge Moor — rhynes come in from both sides with names such as Two Mile Rhyne, Aller Second Rhyne, High Ham Rhyne, Old Greinton Rhyne and Huish Moor Rhyne (3).

Cross straight over the road at Cradle Bridge and go straight on keeping the Drain on the L; more stiles have to be crossed. At Henley Corner turn L on to the lane. Go over Henley Bridge, and go R over the stile. You now follow the River Cary on your R. Go straight on, passing the small, girded Low Ham Bridge. Several gates have to be negotiated on this stretch. At Broadacre Bridge keep the river still on your R.

At the small Pitney Steart Bridge, near a derelict farm on the R, go through the gate, over the track and through the gate ahead to continue on the same side of the River Cary. The river meanders over a broad area of flat land. Stay on the same river bank passing a small but finely-built stone-arched bridge. At Somerton Door Bridge go straight on by negotiating the fencing on the river's edge. Just before Etsome Farm is a smallholding with an orchard running down to the river's edge. Here, go over the stile and then the low wire fence to cross the orchard. Leave via the wire fence and wooden stile. At Etsome Farm go over the stile and the small footbridge to the lane. Go R, and this is the point at which the route leaves the river to head south for Somerton.

The lane crosses the River Cary, and another sluice gate is seen on the L. Go on up the lane for a short distance and take the next lane on the L. Follow the lane round the east side of Bradley Hill, passing the Wessex Water works on the R and the entrance to the Viaduct Trout Fishery on the L. Go up the hill — the only climb since Bawdrip (minus the stiles). At the T-junction go L, staying on the road heading for the railway viaduct. Where the road begins to curve to the R, go L down Cedar Grove. Within 15 yards (metres) go L down the concrete steps, over the stile and bear R along the footpath above the fish ponds. By the railway

Winch, Henley Corner sluice.

go over a stile and through a small gate. At the main road go straight over, heading for the centre of Somerton. Where the road broadens out, go R by the commemorative lamp standing in front of 'The Old Hall'. Go through the wrought-iron gate on the L to enter the churchyard.

1 *The Somerset Levels*

The Somerset moors receive considerable water from the surrounding hills, including the Quantocks, Brendon Hills, the Poldens and Mendips. The area was once an inlet of the sea and the flood plain of five rivers including the Brue, Huntspill and Cary. The Levels were built from sea-deposited clays which restricted the flow of the rivers. The inland area became marsh, fen and bog. The river valleys became filled with peat deposits that contain well-preserved remains from about 4000 BC — including prehistoric trackways and lake villages.

This landscape gave Somerset its name — 'the land of summer' — a fertile land providing grazing for animals in summer, but which was largely covered with water and inaccessible in winter.

2 *King's Sedgemoor Drain*

Work began on cutting the drain in 1794. The old River Cary, which previously meandered across the Levels, entered on to the moor at Henley corner. From here a completely new channel was dug across to the outfall into the River Parrett at Dunball. The value of the land was raised nearly fourfold, because with improved drainage wheat and oats could be sown on the reclaimed land. By 1830 much of the land had been exhausted by overcropping and reverted to rough summer grazing.

In 1939–43 improvements were made to the Drain primarily as a secondary source of water for the Royal Ordnance Factory at Puriton. It was widened and the catchment area was increased to cover an area of some 50,000 acres (20,235 ha). Since then there have been several attempts to grow arable crops, but most of the land is grass pasture supporting dairy cows.

From the moors, embanked rivers flow into the Bristol Channel, which receives high tides — $19\frac{1}{2}$ ft (6 m) above the lowest level in the moors. Water from the moors has to be pumped up into the embanked rivers to prevent permanent flooding. When the tide is at its peak, the rivers are unable to discharge their water so this water has to be stored. During

King's Sedgemoor Drain looking from Greylake Sluice.

Opposite: farm ruin, near Pitney Steart Bridge.

periods of heavy rain the storage is insufficient — the banks are overtopped and widespread flooding occurs. Pumping stations control the water in the rhynes to levels which are best for agriculture, wildlife conservation and other interests. Sluices on many of the rivers and channels control the flow and level.

3   *Wetlands wildlife*

The Somerset Levels and Moors comprise some of the most important wetlands left in England, and are valued for both their unique landscape and the richness and variety of the wildlife.

Winter feeding is a regular occurrence over much of the area, encouraging the over-wintering of birds such as swans, geese, and waders such as lapwing, golden plover, and wildfowl such as teal. Yellow waterlily, or brandy bottle, is quite common on the Drain, where there is a continuous flow of water and a good depth. Perch and pike are to be found — both need to see their prey and consequently avoid muddy waters.

Sedgemoor provides an ideal habitat for amphibious animals, including the common frog (*Rana temporaria*), which can be very abundant in July and August, the common toad (*Bufo vulgaris*) and the natter-jack toad (*Bufo calamita*). The three British species of newt are also present — the crested newt (*Molge cristata*), the smooth newt (*Molge vulgaris*) and the Palmate newt (*Molge palmata*).

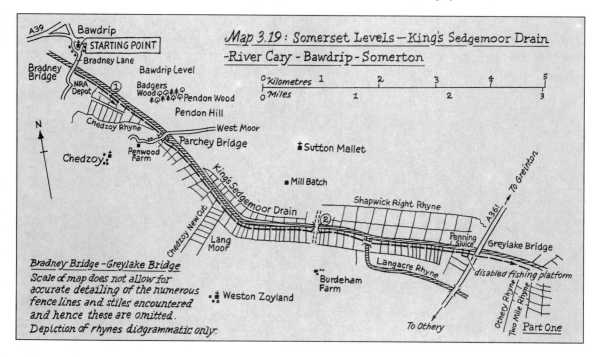

Map 3.19: Somerset Levels — King's Sedgemoor Drain - River Cary - Bawdrip - Somerton

Bradney Bridge - Greylake Bridge
Scale of map does not allow for accurate detailing of the numerous fence lines and stiles encountered and hence these are omitted. Depiction of rhynes diagrammatic only.

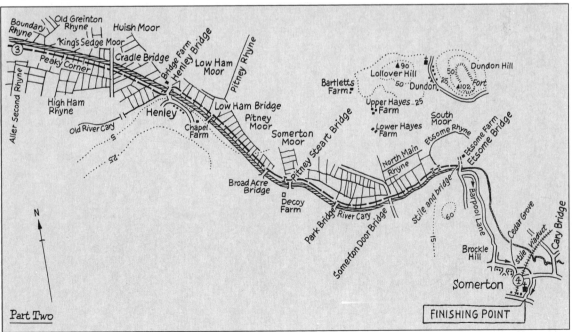

Part Two

FINISHING POINT

ISLES OF SCILLY: ST MARY'S COASTAL WALK

STARTING AND FINISHING
POINT
Hugh Town Quay, St Mary's
(203–902109)
MAP
OS Outdoor Leisure Map
1 : 25 000 Isles of Scilly
LENGTH
14 miles (22.5 km)
ASCENT
Mostly level walking.
NOTE
Dogs are banned from
Porthcressa, Porthmellon and Old
Town beaches from May to
September inclusive.

A coastal walk around the largest island in the Isles of Scilly giving panoramic views of the archipelago. The route encounters superb examples of coastal geomorphological features, the prehistoric past, maritime fortifications and glimpses of present-day island-life realities. Despite its length, this coastal walk is relatively undemanding. Please note that approval in early 1991 to extend the airport runway may mean a diversion of the coastal footpath in the area of Salakee Down/Giant's Castle.

ROUTE DESCRIPTION (Map 3.20)

From the quay at Hugh Town, the hub of island life, turn L at The Mermaid public house. Continue straight on along the road passing the Atlantic Hotel/Inn (L). Where the road forks, at the Corner House, go L. Keep the Green on your R. St Mary's Pool harbour and the old lifeboat station are now in view. At the end of the harbour turn L down the steps (waymarked: 'St Mary's Lifeboat Station') *(1)* and follow the path round.

Take the steps leading up behind the lifeboat station and follow the path to Porth Mellon, a small sandy cove popular with windsurfers. At the road go L past Porthmellon (Industrial) Estate (R) and continue on the path (L) (waymarked: 'Harry's Walls 16th century fort'). Stay on this path for several hundred yards (metres) and then take the steps leading up on the R (waymarked: 'Harry's Walls'). At the lane bear R uphill to the fort, passing a bungalow on the R. From the walls of the sixteenth-century fort are good views over the harbour, and to the twin low peaks of Samson. Bryher, and Carn Near at the southern end of Tresco, can also be seen.

Retrace your steps back to the coastal path, turn R and continue straight on to Thomas Porth, a small cove flanked on the north by Newford Island (accessible at low tide). Pass Porth Loo

Opposite: Peninnis Head — a granite-dominated landscape.

Studio (R) and the terraced cottages (R), and follow the lane passing the small conical peak of Taylor's Island (L). Stay on this lane until it bends sharply R. Just before here go L on the coast path (in the tourist season the beginning of this path may be

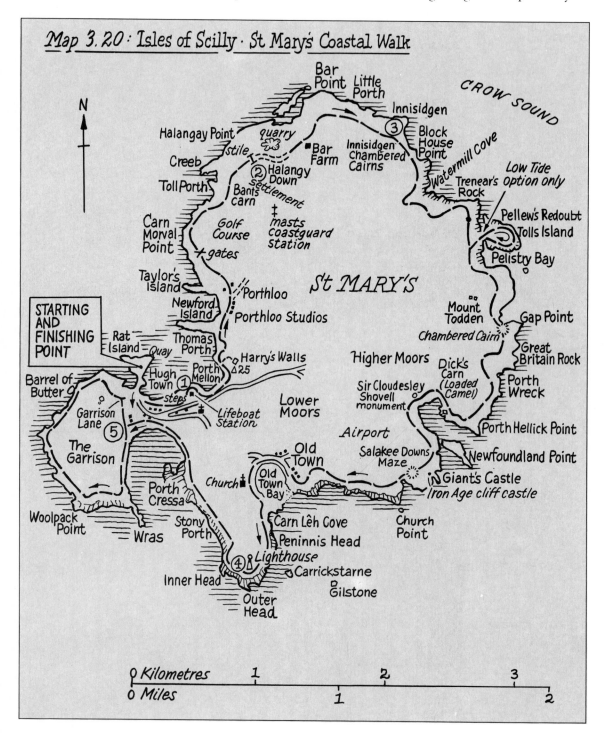

Map 3.20 : Isles of Scilly · St Mary's Coastal Walk

CROW SOUND

N

Bar Point
Little Porth
Innisidgen
③ Block House Point
Halangay Point
quarry
stile
Bar Farm
Innisidgen Chambered Cairns
Watermill Cove
Creeb
② Halangy Down
settlement
Trenear's Rock
Low Tide Option only
Toll Porth
Banis carn
Pellew's Redoubt
Carn Morval Point
Golf Course
masts coastguard station
Tolls Island
gates
Pelistry Bay
Taylor's Island
St MARY'S
Mount Todden
Gap Point
Newford Island
Porthloo
Chambered Cairn
Porthloo Studios
Great Britain Rock
STARTING AND FINISHING POINT
Rat Island
Thomas Porth
Higher Moors
Dick's Carn (Loaded Camel)
Porth Wreck
Quay
Harry's Walls △25
Hugh Town
Porth Mellon
Sir Cloudesley Shovell monument
Porth Hellick Point
Barrel of Butter
① steps
Lifeboat Station
Lower Moors
Newfoundland Point
Garrison Lane
⑤
Airport
Salakee Downs Maze
Giant's Castle
Iron Age cliff castle
The Garrison
Old Town
Church
Old Town Bay
Church Point
Porth Cressa
Woolpack Point
Stony Porth
Carn Lêh Cove
Wras
Peninnis Head
Church Point
Inner Head
④ Lighthouse
Carrickstarne
Gilstone
Outer Head

0 Kilometres | 1 | 2 | 3
0 Miles | 1 | 2

signed 'Juliet's Garden. Food with a View. 20 yds along coastal path'). Pass the tearoom (L) and continue along the path through two wooden gates (please shut). You are now on the golf course and a small notice warns of golf balls and requests that you keep to the course boundaries. The well-defined path here crosses over Carn Morval Point.

At the end of the golf course, with the aerials of the coastguard and radio stations dominating the skyline, the path divides. Take the L fork down towards Toll Porth and the rocky finger of Creeb. At the bottom of the hill a low, iron finger-post points R to Bant's Carn prehistoric burial chamber and ancient village. Halangy Down prehistoric settlement is encountered first. Go up the slope past the remains of the houses, field walls and garden plots, to the chambered cairn with its four massive capstones *(2)*. Retrace your steps down the slope to the track and continue along the track over the hill, keeping farm buildings on the L and aerial masts on the R.

Go over the step-over stile and here, at a small quarry, turn R uphill. Follow the track round to the L (waymarked: 'Innisidgen Burial Chambers'), and to the L at Bar Farm. At Bar Point it is worth leaving the path for the beach and foreshore and the unsurpassed clarity of the waters. At the east end of Bar Point the track divides. Take the L fork (waymarked: 'Innisidgen Burial Chambers') and the superb prehistoric chambered cairns are soon encountered *(3)*.

Continue on the coast path, and on approaching Watermill Cove go down the steps and turn R (L if visiting the beach). Take the first path on the L and at the next path junction (by a seat) bear L, and first L again, dropping down to Trenear's Rock via an old quay. Toll's Island is soon reached. Access to the island can only be gained at low tide. If possible, take the obvious path towards the island's summit and skirt round in a clockwise direction.

Stay on the coast path above Pelistry Bay (beware of offshore breezes here). Continue to Gap Point, a hugely pointed granite headland. A chambered cairn will be seen at the west end of the Point, and the twin-bladed propeller of an experimental vertical axis wind generator on Todden Heath provides a marked cultural contrast. A path can be followed to the far end of the promontory. From here take the lower, seaward path passing Deep Point, and climb up the granite boulder-strewn hill which, in August, is carpeted in flowering heather.

Staying on the path, drop down into Porth Hellick, keeping the tor on the L. This outcrop, Dick's Carn, is colloquially known as 'The Loaded Camel' — the derivation of this name becoming apparent as one looks back from the path at the head

Sub-tropical paradise.

of the beach. Midway along the beach head is a monument of unworked granite to Sir Cloudesley Shovell, whose body was washed ashore here after one of the greatest disasters in British naval history, which occurred in 1707 — some 1500 men lost their lives as part of the British fleet struck rocks off the island.

Stay on the coast path, passing Newfoundland Point and Giant's Castle, the latter being an early Iron-Age cliff castle (L) with low earthworks — the earliest known type of defence on the Islands. A maze of uncertain origin, comprising granite pebbles, can be seen below the north flank of the hill-fort.

The route reaches the airport/heliport, where you should take care to stay on the coast path to Old Town Bay. Pass the Tolman Café (R) and at the road, by the Old Town Café, bear L. Walk along the road for about 100 yards (metres) and then follow the coast path to the old parish church of St Mary's.

From the churchyard continue on the coast path via a stone step-over stile to Carn Lêh and Peninnis Head. At Peninnis Head take the lower path, below the automatic lighthouse, and allow sufficient time to explore this huge sculptured and castellated rockscape where granite outcrops meet the full force of the sea *(4)*.

Staying on the coast path, the route reaches Porth Cressa. Follow the beach to the westernmost end and here turn R down a small alleyway, then L uphill, then first R past the flats. Go L up Garrison Lane. Go through the gateway and you now enter the fortified area known as The Garrison *(5)*. Follow the surfaced road for 50 yards (metres) and take the first L. Immediately on the R is the detention cell and Powder Magazine, which houses an interesting exhibition describing medieval and early Tudor and later fortifications here and elsewhere on the Isles. Follow the Garrison Walls Walk, passing High Battery and Hugh House (the Duchy of Cornwall offices). Continue past Newman House (R) and return to Hugh Town quay via the gateway. Dropping down the hill, turn L at the telephone box.

1   St Mary's Lifeboat Station
The St Mary's Lifeboat Station was re-opened in 1874 after floundering in its earlier years. The first application for provision was made in 1837 and the original vessel was a 12-oared lifeboat housed on Porth Cressa beach. Inside the lifeboat are hand-painted boards detailing the many rescues which the various St Mary's lifeboats have attended. For example, on 23 June 1914, 81 lives were saved from the Red Star Liner SS *Gothland of Antwerp*. There is also a reminder of one of the largest incidents off the British coast — 'Follow-

Opposite: Taylor's Island.

ing the grounding of the tanker *Torrey Canyon* on the Seven Stones on 18 March 1967, the members of the crew, landed at St Mary's, thank the Life-Boat Institution and Hugh Town community for their assistance and very kind hospitality'.

2   *Halangy Village*

Halangy Village (English Heritage) originally dates to about 1700 BC. At about 200 BC the settlement was re-established and remained in use for several centuries. The nearby chambered cairn was the ancestral shrine of the original farming community. At this time the Isles of Scilly were all one large island and the settlement overlooked a wide valley now flanked to the north by the island of Tresco.

Innisidgen burial chambers were probably built some time between 2000 and 1500 BC and stood among fields.

4   *Scilly's ragged coastline*

The Isles of Scilly are comprised of granite some 270–290 million years old. Weathering and attack by the sea have eroded much of the granite, particularly where the rock is soft or along veins or joints. The combination of horizontal and vertical fractures and the erosion on them explains the origin of the many striking features of Scillonian granite. At Peninnis Head the Kettle and Pan Rocks lie some 100 yards (metres) north-west of the lighthouse and have immense rock basins hollowed in them, some as much as 8 ft (2.4 m) across and 6 ft (1.8 m) deep. South of these rocks is the wild rocky inlet enclosed by the outer head of Peninnis, and at the inner head is the partially detached Tooth Rock, some 30 ft (9 m) high. Peninnis Head also comprises the Logan Rock (a huge mass of granite estimated to weigh over 300 tons), two rock faces known as Laughing Man and the Old Witch, and Pulpit Rock, a remarkable example of horizontal decomposition and disintegration of granite.

5   *The Garrison*

The Garrison Walls (English Heritage) were built in their present form between 1715 and 1746. They consist of lengths of curtain wall between artillery bastions providing gun positions. These commanded the seaways and anchorages and the ground immediately beyond the walls. Several batteries today have cannon in position, including 18 pdr English guns of the nineteenth-century on reproduction travelling or garrison carriages. Within the walls were built a guardhouse and barracks, a magazine, a prison and a home for the Master Gunner. The work was carried out largely on the initiative of the then Master Gunner, Abraham Tovey, whose initials can be seen over the gateway entrance.

3·21

DEVON

NORTH WEST DARTMOOR: PREWLEY — KITTY TOR — BRAT TOR — SOURTON TORS

This walk lies entirely outside the Ministry of Defence's Ranges, yet includes some of north Dartmoor's most dramatic views, including the valley of the West Okement River. The walk follows the trackbed of a nineteenth-century peatworks railway for some 2 miles (3.5 km), combining wild landscape with the remains of past human endeavour.

This moderate-length walk is adventurous in places and should not be attempted in poor visibility.

ROUTE DESCRIPTION (Map 3.21)

From parking your vehicle on Prewley Common, walk up the road towards the South West Water treatment works which serve Meldon Reservoir. Where the road bends L by the works entrance follow the boundary wall to the R and continue to follow the wall round in the direction of Sourton Tors. Where the wall bends and drops to the L, continue straight on to pass between two bondstones that are halfway up the hill. At the bondstones bear half-R to the pits and banks of the former Sourton Tors Ice Works *(1)*. Keeping Sourton Tors on your R, continue up to the crest of the col between Sourton Tors and Corn Ridge and then bear half-L for a steep climb to the summit of Corn Ridge. Cut across to a prehistoric cairn and thence to the 'crown' of the ridge — the solitary rock pile of Branscombe's Loaf *(2)*.

Continue almost half-L past the tor to contour round the north-eastern edge of Corn Ridge, thus avoiding the extremely boggy head of the Lyd valley on the R. Aim for the small, unnamed, granite outcrop ahead keeping above (to the R) of a gully on approach. With the three towering rock piles of Black Tor, and with High Willhays, Yes Tor and the West Okement valley upstream, in view, contour half-R to follow the ridge edge round. Keep the West Okement valley well down to your L *(3)*.

Follow a fairly well-defined path, in stretches, to Steng-a-Tor, a small avenue tor. Bad ground lies on the approach and it is

STARTING AND FINISHING POINT

Prewley Moor (191–547909), 4 miles (6.5 km) south-west of Okehampton. Take the A30 from Okehampton, then turn L on to the A386 towards Tavistock. After ½ mile (0.8 km), take the road on the L leading to Prewley Treatment Works (South West Water plc). Go over the cattle grid and follow the road up for about 250 yards (229 m). Park on the R on the common not more than 15 yards (14 m) from the road. Do not park on the road or obstruct vehicular access.

MAP

OS 1 : 25 000 Leisure Sheet 28 — Dartmoor.

LENGTH

10½ miles (17 km)

ASCENT

Three climbs: ½ mile (0.8 km) ascent 351 ft (107 m) to Branscombe's Loaf; ¼ mile (0.4 km) ascent 135 ft (41 m) to Great Links Tor; 1½ miles (2.5 km) gradual ascent 361 ft (110 m) to peat railway looping point on Corn Ridge.

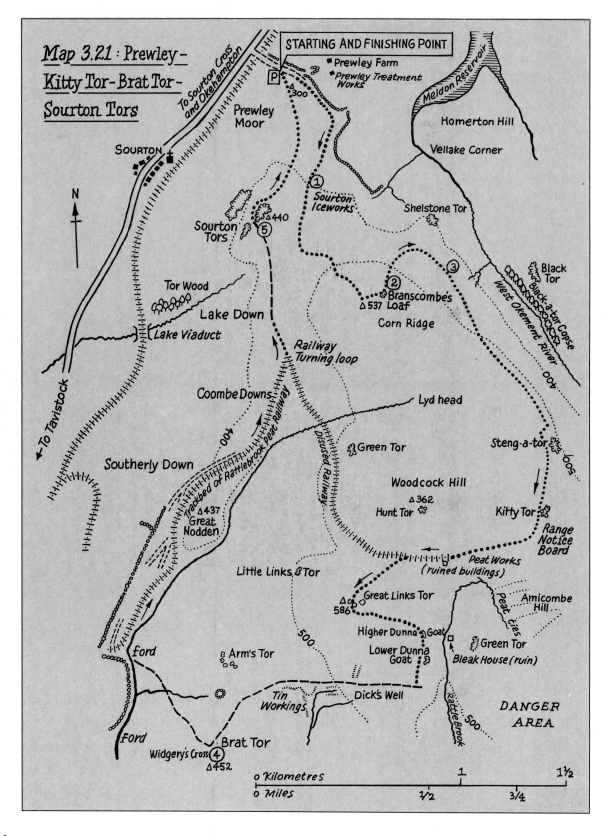

Map 3.21 : Prewley-
Kitty Tor- Brat Tor-
Sourton Tors

STARTING AND FINISHING POINT

To Sourton Cross
and Okehampton

P

Prewley Farm
Prewley Treatment
Works

△ 300

Prewley
Moor

Meldon Reservoir

Homerton Hill

Vellake Corner

SOURTON

N

① Sourton Iceworks

Shelstone Tor

△ 440

⑤

Sourton Tors

Black Tor

③

West Okement River

Black-a-tor Copse

400

Tor Wood

② Branscombe's Loaf

△ 537

Corn Ridge

Lake Down

Lake Viaduct

Railway
Turning loop

Lyd head

Steng-a-tor

500

To Tavistock

Coombe Downs

Trackbed of Rattlebrook Peat Railway

Disused Railway

Green Tor

Woodcock Hill

△ 362

Hunt Tor

Kitty Tor

Southerly Down

400

△ 437
Great
Nodden

Range
Notice
Board

Peat Works
(ruined buildings)

Little Links Tor

Great Links Tor

△
586

Amicombe
Hill

Peat ties

Higher Dunna Goat

Arm's Tor

Lower Dunna
Goat

Green Tor

Bleak House (ruin)

500

ford

Tin
Workings

Dick's Well

Rattlebrook

DANGER
AREA

Ford

Brat Tor

Widgery's Cross ④

△ 452

0 Kilometres	1	1½
0 Miles	½	¾

necessary to bear half-R to avoid this. Keeping R of Okehampton Firing Range boundary poles, head half-R for Kitty Tor. A path makes its way up over dry ground to the L side of the tor — go to the second range pole to pick up this path. From the lookout hut on this small outcrop go half-L for 200 yards (183 m) to a smaller outlying outcrop topped by a Range flagpole.

At the Range noticeboard, by the flagpole, go half-R along a path leading down to the ruined buildings of the Rattlebrook peatworks, which are over-shadowed by Great Links Tor. Keep on this path, to avoid boggy ground in and near the artificial drainage channels on the R. The ruined buildings are a scene of utter desolation — brick, granite blockwork, concrete, iron-work and timber baulks lie in a chaotic jumble, battered con-stantly by the very worst of Dartmoor's weather *(4)*.

From the ruins keep in the same direction, and go up the track of the old peat railway which runs to the R of Great Links Tor. On reaching the cutting, climb up the L side of the track. Great Links Tor comes into view. Follow the track edge for a short distance and then go L on a small path that leads to the tor.

Pass the large, free-standing granite pillar on the side of the tor and turn R to the westernmost pile. Go around the end of the pile and bear half-R to cut across to the two granite outcrops of Higher and Lower Dunna Goat. At Lower Dunna Goat, after climbing on the summit for extensive views up and down the Rattlebrook, keep to the R side of the tor and continue straight on to reach a bridlepath track. Turn R onto the bridlepath and follow to the end of extensive tin cuttings on the L. Here bear half-L following a well-used path to Brat Tor. On the west of the tor is a huge stone cross erected by painter William Widgery in honour of Queen Victoria's Golden Jubilee in 1887. Looking north from the north side of the tor, turn half-L to head down-hill, over a stream, in the direction of the furthest ford over the River Lyd, which lies to the R of a large enclosure and L of two large river bluffs.

Cross the river and bear half-R to cut up the hill. Cross straight over a vehicle track, which leads back down to the river, and, on reaching the second track — the bed of the Rattlebrook peat railway — turn R and follow up over the whale-back dome of Great Nodden and over Coombe Down to the railway turning loop on the slopes of Corn Ridge. Go half-L, cutting down the hill for 75 yards (68 m), turn along a trackway and follow it. Where the track forks, bear L and cross the gert, which plunges into Deep Valley. Continue straight on to Sourton Tors *(5)*. These jagged tors and, if lucky, a setting sun, will cause you to linger before dropping back down to Prewley treatment works (directly ahead), keeping the remains of the ice works on your R.

Sourton Tors from Corn Ridge.

1   *The ice industry*

Before the days of mechanical refrigeration, ice was in great demand for preserving food, particularly among fishmongers in Plymouth. The Sourton Tors Ice Works dates from about 1875 and lasted about 10 years. The site lay between 1300 and 1400 ft (396–426 m) above sea level and here water, a high incidence of frost, exposure to cold winds and easy access for horse and cart, all facilitated the development of this remarkable and unlikely industry.

Water was channelled from a reliable hillside spring into as many as thirty shallow, rectangular pits or ponds in which ice would form during the winter months. The ice was cut into blocks and stored in a nearby granite building, which would have been insulated with earth and turf. In a cool summer the ice supplies would last through to July. The time it took to transport the ice from the works to Plymouth must have meant that considerable wastage occurred.

2   *Branscombe's Loaf*

In the thirteenth century, Bishop Walter Branscombe made many excursions throughout his diocese, which included far-flung places such as Lydford. This often meant traversing the open moors of Dartmoor. On one particular excursion he and his companions fell tired and hungry and on the wind-battered Corn Ridge he was approached by a cloaked stranger on horseback. The stranger offered the Bishop bread and cheese if he would get off his horse, take off his cap, and call him 'Master'. The Bishop almost obliged but, in time it seems, an accompanying servant noticed the stranger's cloven hoof, whereupon the Bishop cried out to God and made the sign of the cross. The stranger instantly vanished, leaving the bread and cheese turned to stone — the granite rock-piles of Branscombe's Loaf.

3   *Black-a-tor Copse*

Black-a-tor Copse (Beare) is the northernmost and highest of the three primeval woodlands on Dartmoor. This pedunculate oak wood covers an area of 14 acres (5.7 ha) on the south-west facing valley-side of the West Okement River, its altitude being 1181–1443 ft (360–440 m). Here the trees reach an age of 100–150 years before they begin to degenerate, which suggests an exceptionally high turnover rate in this severe environment.

4   *Rattlebrook Basin*

The head basin of the Rattlebrook was once the scene of the largest commercial peat cutting on Dartmoor. The first extraction of peat here began in the 1850s. Packhorse transport and then horse-drawn carts conveyed the peat from the

Opposite: Sourton Tors.

moors in those early years. In 1878 the West of England Compressed Peat Company was granted a licence by the Duchy of Cornwall for peat extraction and the construction of a railway. The Rattlebrook Peat Railway, of standard gauge, was completed in 1879. This $5\frac{3}{4}$ mile (9.2 km) long line joined the London and South West Railway near Bridestowe and rises to 1800 ft (549 m) above sea level. No commercial peat cutting takes place on Dartmoor today.

5   *Sourton Tors*

Great Nodden rises to 1434 ft (437 m) above sea level. The entire ridge is of metamorphic slate and rises precipitously from the Dartmoor granite's western boundary on the valley floor of the River Lyd. The massive crags of Sourton Tors are not of granite, but comprise volcanic tuff, baked dolerite and altered agglomerates. Both ridges have been selectively eroded producing marked benched hill slopes.

Ice on Corn Ridge.

3.22

DEVON

SALCOMBE ESTUARY — MALBOROUGH — HOPE COVE — BOLT TAIL — BOLT HEAD

The inland country route enables a coastal walk from Bolt Tail to Bolt Head — a 6-mile (9.6 km) stretch of rugged cliff owned by the National Trust. The area contains excellent diverse bird-watching areas including Soar Mill Cove, Starehole Bottom, Bolberry Down, and soaring cliff faces.

ROUTE DESCRIPTION (Map 3.22)

From the car-park at North Sands go R. Follow the road past South Sands and bear L along the road above Splatcombe Point and continue on to Overbecks Gardens and Museum *(1)*. Pass the ornate main entrance to the Gardens on the L and continue straight on (waymarked: 'Sharp Tor Upper Cliff Path') passing through a small grove of palm trees. At the National Trust cairn go L up the steps and continue on the cliff-top path, passing the OS obelisk (R) marking some 428 ft (130 m) above sea level. Continue straight on, passing above the lichen-clad crags of Sharpitor (L) to Sharp Tor viewpoint.

Stay on the cliff path which runs above Starehole Bay and the valley of Starehole Bottom. At the next footpath junction, go R over the stile (waymarked: 'Soar Mill Cove') and cut straight across the field to the next fingerpost directly ahead. Keep this post on your L and head across the field to a gateway seen to the R of East Soar farmhouse and buildings. In the next field keep to the fence line (L), cross the stile and follow the track keeping the farm buildings on your L (yellow waymarking). Continue on the track passing the telecommunications aerial. At the end of the track, in the National Trust car-park, bear R down the lane passing the terraced cottages (L), which used to be a coastguard station. Ignore the next road junction on the L and continue along the lane. About 88 yards (80 m) beyond the next road junction on the R, turn R down Furzedown Farm road, (waymarked: 'Public Footpath'). This 'open' farm in the season provides cream teas and other refreshments. Almost at the bottom of the farm road go L along a track (yellow waymarking). Keep on the

STARTING AND FINISHING POINT
North Sands car park, just south of Salcombe; fee paying (South Hams District Council). (202–730382). Narrow approach roads — proceed with care, especially in summer months. An alternative inland parking area (National Trust) is available $\frac{1}{2}$ mile (0.75 km) north of Middle Soar (202–713375).
MAPS
OS Outdoor Leisure 1 : 25 000 South Devon for the eastern section of the walk; OS Pathfinder 1362 for the western section.
LENGTH
$13\frac{1}{2}$ miles (21.7 km)
ASCENT
Several coastal climbs including $\frac{1}{2}$ mile (1.2 km) to Overbecks Gardens — 164 ft (50 m); $\frac{3}{4}$ mile (0.8 km) up on to Bolberry Down — 147 ft (45 m); $\frac{1}{2}$ mile (0.8 km) out of Soar Mill Cove — 295 ft (90 m).

Salcombe Castle and Harbour.

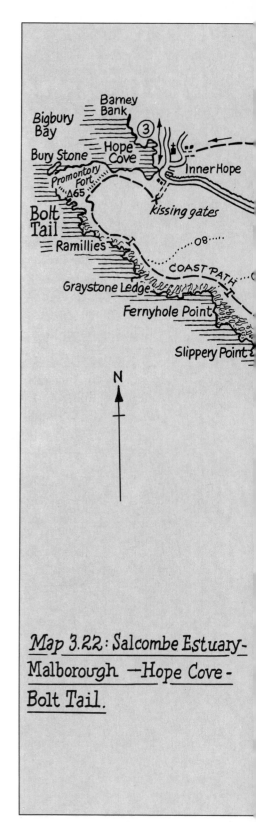

Map 3.22: Salcombe Estuary-
Malborough —Hope Cove-
Bolt Tail.

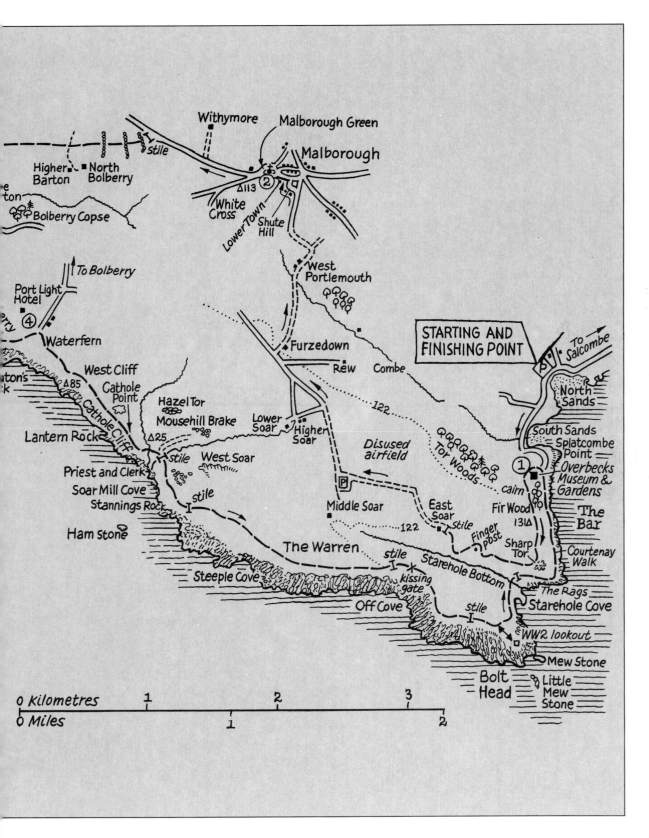

Withymore
Malborough Green
Malborough
stile
Higher Barton
North Bolberry
△113
White Cross
Lower Town
Shute Hill
ton
Bolberry Copse
West Portlemouth

To Bolberry
Port Light Hotel
④
Furzedown
STARTING AND FINISHING POINT
TO Salcombe
Rew
Combe
122
North Sands
Waterfern
West Cliff
Cathole Point
Hazel Tor
Mousehill Brake
Lower Soar
Higher Soar
Disused airfield
122
Tor Woods
South Sands
Splatcombe Point
△85
△25
Overbecks Museum & Gardens
Catbole Cliff
West Soar
cairn
①
Lantern Rock
stile
Fir Wood
The Bar
Priest and Clerk
stile
Middle Soar
East Soar
131△
Soar Mill Cove
Stannings Rock
stile
Finger post
Sharp Tor
Courtenay Walk
Ham stone
The Warren
122
Steeple Cove
stile
Starehole Bottom
The Rags
Starehole Cove
kissing gate
Off Cove
stile
WW2 lookout
Mew Stone
Bolt Head
Little Mew Stone

0 Kilometres   1   2   3
0 Miles   1   2

Hope Cove.

track passing the hamlet of West Portlemouth. The track becomes surfaced here and leads uphill. Where this bends to the R take the public footpath (waymarked) on the L, which leads up towards Malborough Church.

On reaching the road at Malborough *(2)*, continue straight on uphill and then go L down Shute Hill passing the thatched dwellings of Chadders Shute and Shute House (L). At the top of Shute Hill go L past Malborough Primary School. Where you meet the next road (at the top of Lower Town) cross straight over, pass the toilet block on the L, and enter the churchyard. The churchyard is well worth exploring for both its intrinsic value and for the views to the north.

With your back to the church porch (south door), go R along the path to leave the churchyard via a metal gate. Here, at Malborough Green, continue straight ahead from the road junction (signed 'Galmpton/Hope Lane') ignoring the L fork to Bolberry. Go along the lane passing several thatched cottages (R) and the entrance to Withymore Farm (R). Three hundred yards (metres) beyond here, just before the land bends gently to the R, go over the stone stile on the L (broken fingerpost at the time of writing). Continue across the fields (yellow waymarking) sticking to the waymarked route across crop fields.

At the far end of the third field crossed, bear slightly R to go through the top field gate. In the next field cut across to go through the top L gate and then follow the L field boundary to a footpath junction. Continue straight on with field boundaries on your L. The footpath drops down to Inner Hope and from it is a wide vista of the south Devon coast. On approaching Inner Hope keep to the well-defined track for about 200 yards (metres), which then meets a surfaced lane by a bungalow. The small church of St Clements is directly ahead. On reaching the road above the church, cross over and go down the steps. The church (R), a former school house, is simple in its form and content. At the bottom of the steps go R for the Cove (all amenities) and harbour *(3)*.

Retrace the route back to the bottom of the church steps and then follow the road for about 100 yards (metres). Turn R at the junction (waymarked: 'Coast Path Bolt Tail $\frac{1}{2}$ m'). The Lifeboat Station, now disused, is soon reached. Here go R up the steps leading on to the cliff Coast Path to Bolt Tail. This is a National Trust property, and dogs must be kept under proper control. Go through the kissing-gate and keep to the Coast Path to Bolt Tail (avoiding the lower seaward path to the R, which is closed because of landslip/safety reasons) following the yellow arrow

waymarks to and over the earthworks of an Iron-Age promontory fort. This is about 2000 years old and consists of a stone bank with traces of a ditch across the neck of the peninsula.

Follow the path round to the south end of the embankment near a prominent landslip (keep away from the cliff edge) and pass above a place known as Ramillies Cove, named after the wreck of the 90-gun ship of the line which came ashore here in February 1760. Only 26 were saved from a crew of 734. The Coast Path from Bolt Tail to Bolt Head is unfenced to the seaward side for most of its length, and care must be taken. Short marked deviations of the official Coast Path away from the cliff edge must be followed.

The route crosses over Bolberry Down (National Trust) and passes the Port Light Hotel and Restaurant (originally built in 1909 as a club-house for Bolberry Down golf course which closed in 1914) and the Navigation Station (L). From here are good views over the Ham Stone (islet) *(4)*, Stanning Rocks, the Priest and Clerk outcrop and Lantern Rock. This stretch of the Coast Path traverses a ridge between a landlocked valley (L) and the sea, and crosses Waternfern, West Cliff and Cathole Cliff and drops down to Soar Mill Cove.

At Soar Mill Cove, on reaching the footpath junction go over a stile and bear R (waymarked: 'Coast Path Bolt Head 2 m'). Cross the next stile and skirt uphill to the lichen encrusted crags, avoiding the lower path, which is subject to landslips. The path crosses over The Warren and the cliffs above the steeply pitched Off Cove. At Off Cove go over the stile and bear R, then through the kissing-gate to Bolt Head. On Bolt Head bear round to the R to skirt the headland. Linnets, dunnocks, whitethroats and yellowhammers nest among the gorse and bracken. At the next stile continue straight on (waymarked: 'Starehole Bottom, Sharp Tor, Overbecks'). Drop down the hill and at the path junction near the bottom go R for the World War II lookout. Retrace your steps and continue on the Coast Path round to Starehole Cove. Starehole Cove and Bottom are of great ecological interest. The area is famed for its butterflies and lies on migration routes for many birds and insects.

From the cove, cross the stile and continue on the Coast Path (waymarked: 'Coast Path Overbecks $\frac{3}{4}$ m'). This lower track is known as the 'Courtenay Walk' and was cut by order of one of the Earls of Devon for those who love wildness and solitude. Continue on the path — with views north over Salcombe and its estuary, and east to Prawle Point. Go through the wood and on reaching a rough road continue straight on passing several houses on your R. At the road junction bear R and follow the road down to South Sands and North Sands.

Opposite: Malborough from West Portlemouth.

1 *Overbecks Gardens and Museum*

Overbecks Gardens is a twentieth-century creation begun by Mr Edric Hopkins in 1901. In 1913 the property was sold to Mr G. M. Vereker, who developed the garden further. On his death in 1928 the property was sold to Mr Otto Christop Joseph Gerhardt Ludwig Overbecks, previously a research chemist who had invented a non-alcoholic beer. He carried on the tradition of adding rare plants. On his death in 1937 the house and garden were left to the National Trust 'for use as a park and museum and a hostel for youth'.

Overbecks House contains a museum which includes an interesting maritime collection reflecting the history of Salcombe as a prosperous port and nineteenth-century ship-building town.

2 *Malborough*

Malborough sits on a schist plateau some 400 ft (122 m) above sea level. All Saint's Church, known as 'the Cathedral of the South Hams', is a landmark over a wide landscape. The existing building appears to have been founded in about AD 1200 and considerable restoration was carried out in the fifteenth century.

3 *Hope Cove*

Hope Cove was an important refuge for sailing ships — on 3 September 1855 it was recorded that 50 to 60 vessels were at anchor here. As well as offering a safe haven, the community was engaged in a variety of maritime activities, including fishing, lifeboat and coastguard services and smuggling. Coastguards came into prominence in about 1825 and soon brought an end to smuggling which, together with the pillaging of wrecks, was an important means of supplementing income.

4 *The Ham Stone*

The Ham Stone is associated with a once-common saying — if a married couple remained childless for some length of time, the husband should be told to go and dig up the Ham Stone with a wooden pickaxe. The way in which this could have helped is best left to the imagination!

3·23

SOMERSET

THE QUANTOCK HILLS: NETHER STOWEY – RAMS COMBE – BICKNOLLER POST – HOLFORD

The Quantock Hills form a compact upland stretching for some 12 miles (19 km) above the vale of Taunton Deane to the Bristol Channel. They rarely extend to 4 miles (6.4 km) wide. These hills are ideal walking country and this adventurous walk explores summit, ancient trackways, wooded combes, and two villages that both have strong links with William and Dorothy Wordsworth and Samuel Taylor Coleridge. It is important on the Quantocks to guard against fires, and please keep dogs under close control.

ROUTE DESCRIPTION (Map 3.23)

At the Clock Tower next to the site of the former village gaol go up Castle Street. Continue on up the street passing the Library/Museum and Quantocks Information Centre on the R. At the road junction, go straight on up Castle Hill (highway signed: 'Over Stowey/Crowcombe'). Within 55 yards (50 m) go R up Butcher's Lane, which skirts around the site of Stowey Castle. Just before the next road junction go L over the right-hand stile (waymarked; 'Public Footpath'). Dogs must be kept on leads. This path makes its way around Stowey Castle. Keep the stream down to your R. Go over a stile and the Norman castle's mound and ramparts are seen on the L. At the lane go over the stile ahead or take the L stile if wanting to visit the castle site before starting out on the main part of the walk.

Turn R down the lane. Pass a few houses and then turn L down the dead-end Hockpitt Lane. At Hockpitt Farm keep the barn conversion on your L and the farmhouse on your R and continue straight on over a stile. Go through the next gate and follow the R field hedge up to the top corner of the field. Here, with a good view back over Stowey Castle, go over the two stiles and continue straight on, keeping the field hedge on your R. On approaching Cross Farm, Over Stowey church tower can be seen ahead. At the lane go over the stile and at the lane T-junction go straight on along the lane.

STARTING AND FINISHING POINT
There are several places from which this walk can begin, depending on the time of year. Avoid parking in Holford and Nether Stowey villages during peak holiday times. The walk described begins at Nether Stowey, 7 miles (11 km) to the north-west of Bridgwater, just off the A39 Minehead road. Avoid parking in the main streets. The walk begins at the Clock Tower (191–192397). Other parking areas include: Forestry Commission car-park at Rams Combe (191–165378); Crowcombe Park Gate (191–151378); Holford village green car-park (191–155410).
MAPS
Ordnance Survey Pathfinder 1 : 25 000 1216 Watchet.
LENGTH
13½ miles (21.7 km)
ASCENT
Main climbs: ¾ mile (1.2 km) Rams Combe to Crowcombe Park Gate 328 ft (100 m); ¾ mile (1.2 km) Lady's Combe to Dowsborough.

You soon reach the clustered village of Over Stowey. St Peter and St Paul parish church, with its fourteenth-century tower, is worth visiting. Stay on the lane, passing the Old School House on your L. Within a few yards, by the Over Stowey Village Hall Committee's private car-park, go R through a small kissing-gate (waymarked: 'Public Footpath'). Cut diagonally across the field to another kissing-gate. At the lane turn R, following a stream running alongside a broad, well-maintained hedgerow. At the next lane junction go R keeping the Guide and Scout hut on your L.

The lane leads over a landscape of woods and forests, field and combe to Adscombe Farm (L). Where the road bends to the R, go straight on along the track (Forestry Commission waymarking: 'To Quantock Forest Trail'). At the cattle grid go through the gate, and go straight on keeping the river down on your L. Pass Great Wood Camp (L) with its uniform chalet accommodation. There is a steady climb for a short while and soon a small Forestry Commission car-park is encountered on the L. At an isolated cottage, where Quantock Combe drops down to meet Rams Combe, stay on the track keeping the cottage on your L.

Keep to this track up Rams Combe, passing a Forestry Commission hut and toilet block on the L and a picnic site to the R. Please remember that this is a working forest — smokers beware, and do not approach men/machines at work. Go straight on and you soon reach a small label by a suffering old oak tree denoting the sad loss of most of the ancient broadleaf forest of Quantock. Where the track bends sharply to the R to the parking area, go straight on keeping the headstream on your L. The track becomes traffic-free except for the occasional Forestry Commission vehicle. You may well hear the mewing of a buzzard as you climb out of Rams Combe to the end of the forestry plantation.

Go through the gate and continue on the track, which now crosses open country to Crowcombe Park Gate (parking available). During the lambing season dogs must be kept under close control. Cross the lane and head up over the crest of the hill along a broad track. Stay on this track along the ridge, keeping 'The Lodge' dwelling and hedgebank/fenceline on the L. Hurley Beacon, at 1158 ft (353 ml) above sea level with its prehistoric cairn can be seen to the L. A path leads off the ridge track via a stile (L) to this superb viewpoint. From here you can see a good stretch of the Quantock Hill range *(1)*. Retrace your steps to the ridge track and go L.

At Halsway Post, with Halsway Combe dropping steeply down to the L, take the R fork over Thorncombe Hill. Pass Lowsey Thorn above Slaughterhouse Combe. The massive box buildings of Hinkley Point Nuclear Power Station can be seen

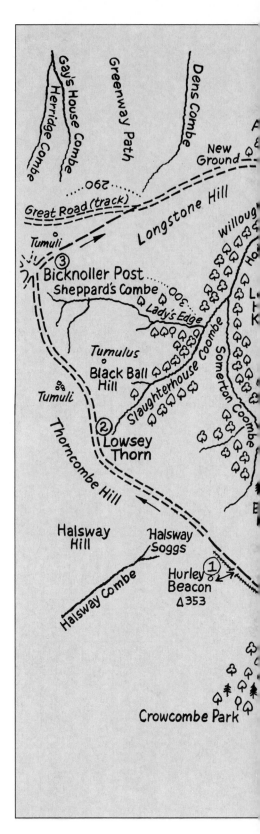

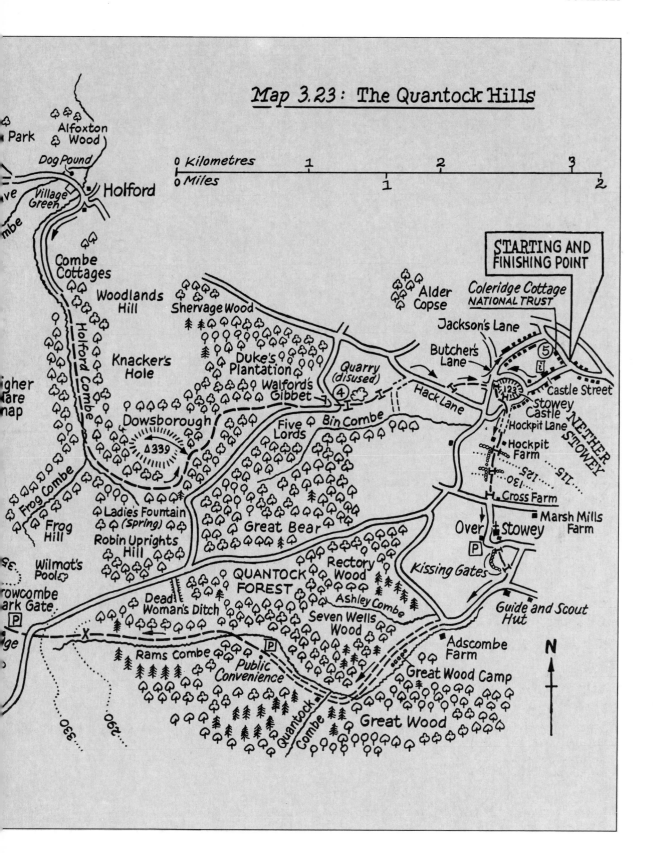

Map 3.23 : The Quantock Hills

from this point — an Area of Outstanding Natural Beauty gives way to an area of outstanding natural concern *(2)*. Stay on the track over Black Ball Hill, passing a fair-sized prehistoric cairn on your L. You may see glimpses of red deer on the hills *(3)*. From Bicknoller Post go R along the broad track, and where this divides take the L fork, keeping a small prehistoric cairn to your L. At the next track divide, take the L fork, which heads down in the direction of the nuclear power station. The track soon meets the broad track known as 'The Great Road', believed to be an old coach road, above the unwooded Dens Combe. Go R here. On approaching New Ground wood take the R fork. A waymarking post is encountered — keep straight on (waymarked: 'Holford'). Within 33 yards (30 m) another post is encountered. Here take the path waymarked 'Holford' leading off into the top part of the wood. Keep on the bridlepath, and on the L you can see Alfoxton Park, home to the Wordsworths at the end of the eighteenth century.

On reaching the metalled lane, the route passes an ancient dog pound on the L. From here ignore the turning to the L and continue straight on down the lane passing Holford village green (R). At the next bend in the road, by a row of thatched cottages, go R along a rough track that meets a metalled lane. Here go R (highway signed: 'Holford Combe No Through Road'). Or, turn L here for the small village.

Continue on the lane in Holford Combe passing a large hotel and Combe Cottages on the R. In the wood keep on the bridleway, which crosses the river in several places via a series of fords.

At Frog Combe, which drops down from the R, cross the small river and go straight on up Lady's Combe via another ford. There is a gradual and then a steep climb up the valley. At the head of this combe is a bridlepath T-junction. Here go L uphill to the next bridlepath junction. Going L here brings you on to the northern ramparts of Dowsborough prehistoric hill-fort, with good views all round. Retrace your steps to the bridlepath T-junction and then go straight on, on the bridlepath, ignoring the small path dropping down to the L. Quantock ponies are often seen wintering in these woods.

At the next cross tracks turn L, staying on the bridlepath down through the wood. On reaching a beech-lined boundary bank, go R along the track. At the lane, by Five Lords overlooking Bin Combe, go L and follow the wood-lined lane down. Walford's Gibbet is soon reached *(4)*. At the point where the lane bends sharply to the L, go over the stile leading into a field on the R. Cut across the field, which offers views over the Bristol Channel. Ahead lies Nether Stowey. The route skirts above a small disused quarry pit, and from here keep the field boundary on your R.

Opposite: Thorncombe Hill from near Bicknoller Post.

Keep the same line in the next field. Cross the stile midway down this field and go L along a green lane. At the surfaced lane go R. Just before this lane drops down, go L over a stile (waymarked: 'Public Footpath'), keeping the fence line on your L. At the point where the field boundary swings away to the L continue straight on in the direction of the castle mound. If starting this walk from elsewhere and not wanting to visit the village, go R on to Butcher's Lane to take the R of the two immediate stiles (waymarked) to skirt around Stowey Castle. Otherwise, continue straight on, ignoring Butcher's Lane, and at the junction with Jackson's Lane, take the R fork. Follow this road to the T-junction and then go R. Coleridge Cottage (National Trust) is passed on R *(5)*. The Clock Tower marks the end of the walk but, if starting from elsewhere, go R up Castle Street.

1   *Quantock Hills*
    The rocks of the Quantock inlier belong to the Devonian period, and are some 350–400 million years old. The oldest rocks are known as Hangman Grits — mainly hard, quartzitic sandstones — and these form much of the higher moorland and afforested ground in the north Quantocks. The central hills comprise the Ilfracombe Beds — sandstones, slates and limestones — and the southern end consists of Morte Slates — the youngest rocks of the Quantocks.

2   *The Quantocks heritage*
    The heathland and oakwoods of the Quantocks are nationally important wildlife habitats, and over 6000 acres (2500 ha) are notified as Sites of Special Scientific Interest. There are 48 nationally important Scheduled Ancient Monuments on the hills, together with some 360 identified archaeological sites. In 1957, 38 sq miles (99 sq km) of the Quantocks was designated as an Area of Outstanding Natural Beauty — the first such area in England. The designation reflects Government recognition of the area as a landscape of national importance.

3   *Staghunting*
    Staghunting began on the Quantocks in about 1861, when a number of Exmoor deer were brought to the hills by Mr Fenwick Bissett. The first Quantock stag was killed in August 1865. The activity arouses strong feelings. In 1949 a Government Committee was set up 'to inquire into practices or activities which may involve cruelty to British Wild Mammals for purposes of sport or food'. At that time, and since,

The Quantock Hills — England's first designated Area of Outstanding Natural Beauty.

Walkers on Hurley Beacon.

only by hunting, say its supporters, can the number of deer be safely and responsibly controlled. The introduction overnight to legislate against such activity would no doubt have consequences on the social fabric of the area and would produce a vacuum for adequate deer management. Perhaps the solution would be to introduce legislation banning the activity (on moral grounds at least), but identifying a realistic period for all parties to adapt.

4 *Walford's Gibbet*

Walford's Gibbet marks the site where, in the eighteenth century, John Walford — a local charcoal-burner — was hanged after murdering his wife in a rage. After hanging for the usual time, the body was taken down, put into an iron cage and suspended on the gibbet, where it stayed for exactly twelve months after he committed the murder. His body was buried the next day 10 ft (3 m) deep, beneath the gibbet.

5 *Samuel Taylor Coleridge*

Samuel Taylor Coleridge, his wife and baby, made their home in Nether Stowey from about 1797 to 1800, following his friendship with a local man, Thomas Poole. While living at the cottage in Lime Street, he wrote all or part of *The Rime of the Ancient Mariner*, *Christabel* and *Frost at Midnight*. Six months after moving into the cottage he visited William Wordsworth and his sister Dorothy, who were living rent-free at Racedown, West Dorset. The lives of the two poets intertwined, particularly after the Wordsworths went to live at Alfoxton (Alfoxden) at Holford in 1797–8.

Among William Wordsworth's pieces composed at Alfoxton are *Ruth*, *The Thorn*, *The Whirlwind from behind the Hill*, and his *A Night Piece*, which describes an imposing company of clouds gathered about a brilliant winter moon observed on a walk from Nether Stowey back to Holford.

3·24

DEVON

HARTLAND POINT — SPEKE'S MILL MOUTH — DIXON'S WELL — STOKE

Situated in the remote north-west corner of Devon, this circular route follows the bulk of Hartland's coast, encountering some of the most spectacular coastal scenery in Britain. Cliffs and beaches should be walked with care. Cliffs can be unstable in places — keep to the waymarked 'Coast Path'. Beaches are usually covered by the sea at high tide. The return route inland follows quiet country lanes, green lanes and public paths over Hartland plateau.

ROUTE DESCRIPTION (Map 3.24)

From the car-park at Blagdon Farm near Hartland Point, take the Coast Path westwards around the cliff to a small white building. Go up by the side of it and through the gateway (waymarked: 'Coastpath'). Keep the coastguard station and aerial on your R. A wreck in the cove can be seen from here, but do not venture too close to the cliff edge. Continue on the Coast Path crossing two stiles. Hartland Point lighthouse can be seen to the north *(1)*. Crossing two more stiles, you will encounter the first of several waterfalls along the coastline. Here, bear L and follow the stream (Titchberry Water) for several hundred yards (metres). Cross the footbridge on the R over the stream and follow the Coast Path uphill and round to the R. At the next path junction continue straight on over a stile. You are now on the level ground known as 'Smoothlands'. A small detour from the Coast Path to Damehole Point offers extensive views of the Devon and Cornwall coastline southwards and of Lundy Island to the north.

Retrace your steps to the Coast Path and make the steep ascent to the cliff top. At the next path junction continue over Blegberry Cliff and then tack carefully down into the valley bottom of Blegberry Water. Cross the small arched stone bridge — a small path leading off immediately on the R leads to a viewpoint above another small waterfall.

Continue on the waymarked Coast Path that leads away from the cliff edge. Cross another stile and drop down into the Abbey

STARTING AND FINISHING POINT
Car-park (small charge) at Blagdon Farm, Hartland Point, 9 miles (14.5 km) west-north-west of Clovelly (190–235275). From Hartland village, follow road signs for Lighthouse/Hartland Point.
MAP
OS 1 : 25 000 Pathfinder Series Sheet SS 22/32
LENGTH
16 miles (25.7 km)
ASCENT
Some demanding coastal stretches involving short, steep climbs and descents, including the climb out of Titchberry Water valley, the climb on to Blegberry Cliff, the drops into Blegberry Water and Abbey River valleys, and the climb up Swansford Hill. Inland two uphill climbs: out of Lymebridge, and to Berry.

valley, taking care on the descent. Pass the cottage (R) and then immediately go R through a kissing-gate (waymarked: 'Coast Path') and cross the bridge over the lively and tree-lined river. A prominent ruin, known as 'the Pleasure House' is soon encountered on Warren Cliff. Continue over Warren Cliff (where rabbits were once bred in artificial burrows) and at its far end keep the Rocket House on your L. Pass this building, cross the stile and bear R to drop down to Hartland Quay *(2)*. From the hotel follow the public footpath leading off from the R at the bottom of the road; after a short climb you re-gain the Coast Path.

You soon reach the half-domed isolated hill of St Catherine's Tor. Another small waterfall will be seen on the north side of the hill. Go over a stile here, and continue straight on, crossing the concrete stepping-stones on the way. From the stepping stones take the L fork path to a gate. Through the gate, bear R along the Coast Path. Cross the ladder-stile further on and the route then drops down Speke's Mill Mouth. Near the bottom of the hill a path leads off to the R to another fine rock-sculptured beach. Continue on the Coast Path for a remarkable waterfall ahead — the finest of the coastal waterfalls on the north Devon coast *(3)*.

From the waterfall follow the Milford Water upstream to a footbridge, and cross here. Continue up Swansford Hill, which involves a steep climb. Go over the next stile and continue on the Coast Path on the edge of the remote Milford Common. Off Gunpath Rock the remains of the *Green Ranger*, wrecked in November 1962, may be seen, depending on the tide. Above Dixon's Well the Coast Path veers inland. Stay on the path and leave the field by way of a wooden gate. Here at the crossroads the route now swings northwards (L) for the return to Blagdon Farm. Stay on the lane to the small hamlet of Elmscott. At Elmscott Crossroads (by Elmscott Farm), go L along the lane (signed: 'Stoke/Hartland') passing the Youth Hostel (L). At the telephone box take the footpath directly ahead leading up a flight of steps alongside the cottage. Enter the field (no stile) and keep to the L field boundary to the gate ahead. On reaching the lane continue straight on to the unspoilt hamlet of Milford. Drop down the lane passing Docton Mill (R), restored in 1980.

At Lymebridge, by the delightful thatched Speke's Valley cottages, go L up the hill (signed: 'Stoke/Hartland'). The ascent is steep in this peaceful wooded combe. Continue past the entrance to Ackworthy and Trellick to Kernstone Cross. At Kernstone Cross continue straight on (signed: 'Unsuitable for Motors'). Keep Wargery Farm on your R and continue along the track. At the next crosstracks go straight on down the metalled lane to Stoke. At the main road go L and enter the churchyard. St Nectan church deserves exploring *(4)*.

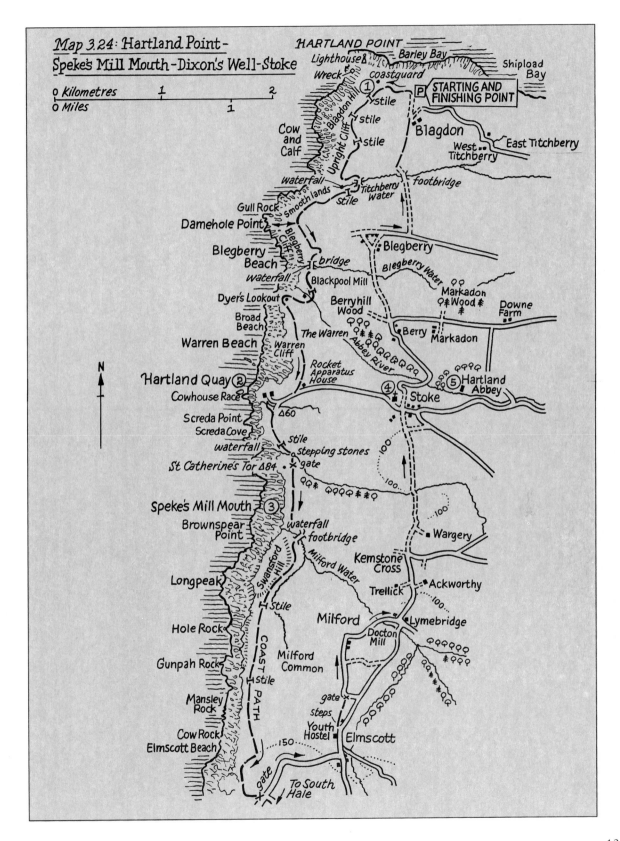

Map 3.24: Hartland Point -
Speke's Mill Mouth - Dixon's Well - Stoke

Hartland Point.

Looking south from near Blagdon Farm.

Leave the churchyard at the eastern end via the lower path on the north side of the church. Go over the stone stile and turn L down the lane, soon passing the site of the medieval fish pond (R) and Hartland Abbey *(5)*. Over the river the lane climbs steeply to Berry.

Past Berry Farm take the metalled green lane directly ahead for Blegberry. On approaching Blegberry, bear R up the track just before the farm, passing several cottages on your R. At the road turn R and follow for several hundred metres to a green lane on the L (waymarked: 'To Public Bridleway'). Go down this green lane passing through a shrubby enclave. At the bottom of the combe cross the footbridge and follow the track up and to the R for Blagdon Farm and the car-park.

1   *Hartland Point*
    Ptolemy of Alexandria in Roman times referred to 'Hercules Promontory', and there are those who think he was alluding to Hartland Point. The cliffs here are 350 ft (106.5 m) high, and perched below is the much-needed lighthouse erected in 1874. The surveyor was unable to get to the site and his plans had to be made from observations and measurements taken from a ship at sea. For over 100 years the light was manned by three keepers living with their families in adjoining accommodation. In 1963 the light was completely automated. The keepers were withdrawn and their quarters were demolished, making way for a helicopter landing-site. The foghorn can be heard for $5\frac{1}{2}$ miles (9 km) — one of the most powerful in the British Isles.

2   *Hartland Quay*
    Hartland Quay was built in the fifteenth century, largely to serve the local coastal trade in grain, coal, lime and building materials such as planks, slate and nails. The first recorded evidence of its use is found in Hartland Church Accounts for 1602, when lime was purchased. In the 1820s, at the height of the quay's prosperity, Edward Hockin formed the Hartland Quay Bank, which produced its own £1 and £5 notes.

    The quay was breached several times by storms in the nineteenth century, and in 1887 the pierhead was swept away. The remainder was destroyed in a gale on 8 October, 1896. It was never replaced due to a decline in coastal trade. A museum, housed on the upper floor of the cottages, contains a fascinating display relating local maritime history. Open daily during the summer.

3   *Milford Water*
    At Speke's Mill Mouth, Milford Water hangs some 157 ft (48 m) above sea level and reaches the beach in a series of

Opposite: waterfall, Speke's Mill Mouth.

waterfalls, the largest unbroken fall being 54 ft (16.5 m). This is a structurally-controlled waterfall, where the route it takes is determined by the local geological structure.

4   *St Nectan Church*

The parish church of Hartland, at Stoke, has been described as 'the Cathedral of North Devon' due to its situation, size and beauty. The present church, patron St Nectan, was built by Countess Gytha (mother of King Harold) as a thanks-offering for the safe return of her husband, Earl Godwin, from a storm off the coast. The present church contains an outstanding roof and that part adjoining the chancel is a striking feature, being panelled and vividly decorated with large painted stars. The Lady Chapel contains one of the finest roofs of its kind and comprises fourteenth-century bosses. The massive unrestored oak rood screen, $45\frac{1}{2}$ ft (14 m) in length, dates to the late fifteenth century. There is a small museum in the priest's room (the 'Pope's Chamber') over the north porch. Stranger's Hill, at the western end of the churchyard, contains the burials of many local shipwreck victims.

5   *Hartland Abbey*

Hartland Abbey is an eighteenth- to nineteenth-century mansion incorporating the cloisters of an Augustinian abbey that was founded in the twelfth century. It was consecrated in 1160 and remained an abbey until 1539, the last in the country to be dissolved by Henry VIII. The bulk of the abbey property in the parish was granted to William Abbott, 'Sergeant of the Cellar', or Chief Butler to Henry VIII. The Stucley family have owned the abbey since 1824.

4.25

SOMERSET

EXMOOR: HORNER – DUNKERY BEACON – STOKE PERO – BOSSINGTON – HURLSTONE POINT – SELWORTHY BEACON – ALLERFORD

This figure-of-eight walk covers the quintessence of Exmoor's landscape — a mixture of rolling moorlands, to include Exmoor's highest point, wooded combes, meadows, dramatic coastline, and several unspoilt villages. The walk lies almost totally within the National Trust's Holnicote Estate. This demanding walk can be broken in half into two moderate-more strenuous routes.

ROUTE DESCRIPTION (Map 4.25)

From the toilet block in the car-park go R along a small path leading to a lane. Turn L up this lane passing a three-storey converted watermill. Near the top of the hill go R along the track (waymarked: 'Webber's Post/Dunkery Beacon'), going through a large gate. The track runs along the east flank of the wood up towards Chapel Steep. Soon the track divides — continue along the R ungated fork. This is quite a steep climb up through the wood. At the next cross tracks, continue on uphill (ungated). The track begins to level out — ignore the path coming in from the R. The track soon runs parallel with and meets the road leading up to Webber's Post.

Continue on up the lane and at the next road junction take the L fork (highway signed: 'Dunkery Beacon/Wheddon Cross'). Stay on this lane with the domed Luccombe Hill on your L. Pass the finger-post on the L ('Dunster Path to Brockwell'). Climb steeply up the lane, going round a bend to the L, and at about 148 yards (135 m) beyond this point go R along the path waymarked: 'Dicky's Path to Stoke Ridge'. Now for some level walking.

The track contours its way over the steep defile of Hollow Combe. Midway between Hollow Combe and Aller Combe turn up the broad path which leads off on the L up to Dunkery Beacon. Where the path begins to level out, at the track junction go R for Dunkery Beacon (1). The hardest climbs are now accomplished until Hurlstone Combe.

STARTING AND FINISHING POINT
National Trust car-park in Horner village (181–897454), $1\frac{1}{2}$ miles (2.5 km) south-west of Porlock. Follow signs to West Luccombe and Horner from the A39.
MAP
OS Pathfinder Series 1 : 25 000 1215 Minehead.
LENGTH
$16\frac{1}{2}$ miles (26.5 km).
ASCENT
5 steep climbs: 1 mile (1.6 km) Horner to Webber's Post 574 ft (175 m); $\frac{1}{2}$ mile (0.8 km) Webber's Post to Dicky's Path 131 ft (40 m); 1 mile (1.6 km) Dunkery Hill to Dunkery Beacon 590 ft (180 m); $\frac{1}{4}$ mile (0.4 km) West Lynch to Bossington Hill 164 ft (50 m); $\frac{3}{4}$ mile (1.2 km) up Hurlstone Combe 525 ft (160 m).

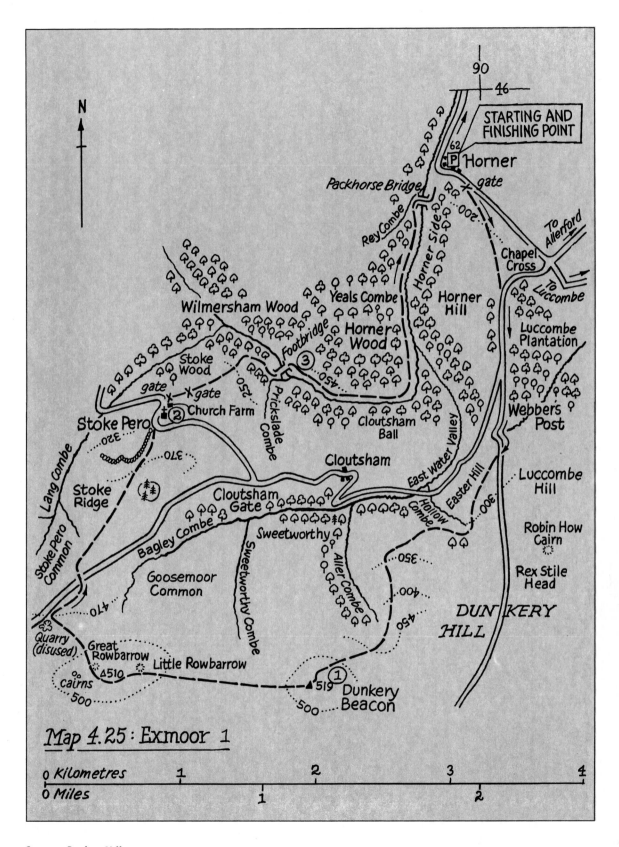

90
46
STARTING AND
FINISHING POINT

62
P Horner

Packhorse Bridge
gate
To Allerford

Rey Combe
Horner Side
Chapel Cross
To Luccombe

Wilmersham Wood
Yeals Combe
Horner Hill
Luccombe Plantation

Footbridge
Horner Wood
③

Stoke Wood
gate gate
250
Webber's Post

Stoke Pero
② Church Farm
Prickslade Combe
Cloutsham Ball

320
Cloutsham
East Water Valley
Luccombe Hill

Lang Combe
370
Stoke Ridge

⚘

Cloutsham Gate
Bagley Combe
Sweetworthy
Easter Hill
300
Robin How Cairn

Stoke Pero Common
Sweetworthy Combe
Hollow Combe
Rex Stile Head

Goosemoor Common
Aller Combe
350
DUNKERY HILL

470
400

450

Quarry (disused)
Great Rowbarrow
Little Rowbarrow

cairns
△510
500

①
▲519
Dunkery Beacon
500

Map 4.25 : Exmoor 1

| 0 | Kilometres | 1 | 2 | 3 | 4 |

| 0 | Miles | 1 | 2 |

From the beacon go westwards along a well-defined track heading along the ridge to Little and Great Rowbarrow. The prehistoric ridge cairn of Little Rowbarrow (L) is passed first. The next cairn is Great Rowbarrow. From here continue on the broad track north-west, ignoring the path on the L leading through the heather to a small group of cairns.

Stay on the track, which offers a view over Wilmersham Common and Babe Hill. By the road go R along a grass track running parallel with the road. This track soon narrows to a path. On approaching the delightful Bagley Combe go L to meet the lane. Strike quarter-L across the open moor on a well-defined path heading in the direction of a clump of pine trees surrounding a small enclosure on Stoke Ridge. This path passes to the L of the enclosure. Ahead, across the combe, is Wilmersham Farm. The path crosses an area of leggy gorse, following a beech hedgebank on the L. On reaching the lane go L downhill. Within a short distance you arrive at Stoke Pero parish church – the most isolated and highest church on Exmoor at 1013 ft (308 m) above sea level *(2)*. Some 100 years ago, about twelve cottages stood in the area.

Below the church is Church Farm. Here go R through the gateway and head up through the small farmyard to the gate ahead. Through the gate, continue on the enclosed bridlepath. At the end of this track go through the gate, and go straight on keeping the fenceline and wood on the L. Before reaching the end of this field stay on the bridlepath waymarked 'Horner' and then enter Stoke Ford via a gate. The bridlepath drops steeply down through the wood to Horner Water. Ignore all side paths/tracks until reaching the valley bottom.

Where Prickslade Combe waters tumble down to the Horner valley, cross the Horner Water via the footbridge *(3)*. From the footbridge turn R along the track heading downstream.

On approaching Horner go R over the packhorse bridge and follow the track to the lane. Go R for the car-park if wishing to do the Hurlstone Point-Selworthy Beacon section of the walk on another day; or go R if wanting to stop at the Horner Tea Garden and Gift Shop. Otherwise, follow the lane to West Luccombe. Go over the road bridge and, at the road junction, go straight on (signed: 'Porlock/Minehead'). At the point where this lane bends to the L go straight on along a track (waymarked: 'A39 Road/Bossington'). Enter the meadow via a gate and go straight on keeping the river on your R. Dogs must be kept on a lead.

At the A39, by New Bridge, go R over the road bridge and then immediately L over a stile (waymarked: 'Bossington'). Keep to the L field boundary following the river downstream. On the R are the broadleaf wooded slopes of Allerford Plantation and the

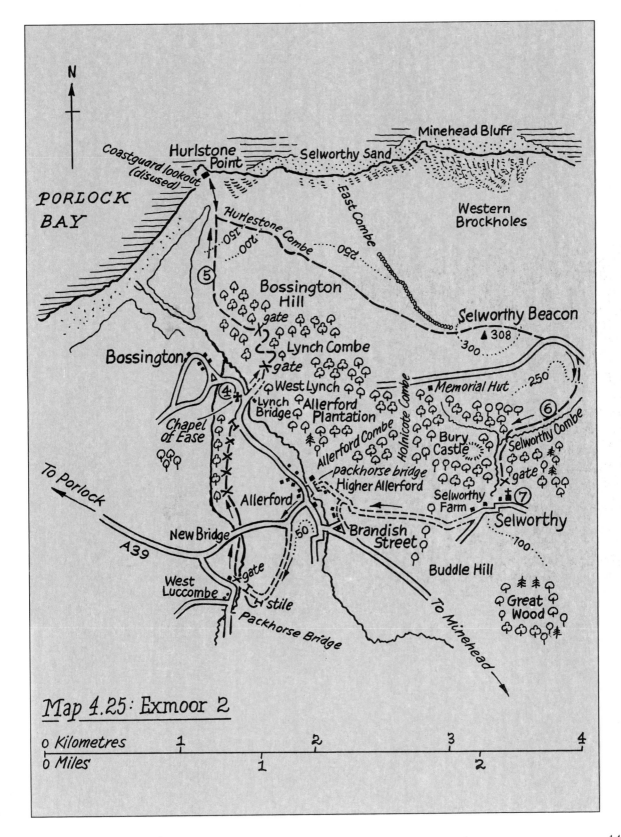

N

PORLOCK BAY

Coastguard lookout (disused)

Hurlstone Point

Minehead Bluff

Selworthy Sand

Western Brockholes

Hurlstone Combe

East Combe

⑤

150

200

250

Bossington Hill

Selworthy Beacon

gate

▲ 308

300

Lynch Combe

gate

West Lynch

Bossington

Memorial Hut

250

⑥

△

④

Lynch Bridge

Allerford Plantation

Holnicote Combe

Selworthy Combe

Chapel of Ease

Allerford Combe

Bury Castle

gate

To Porlock

packhorse bridge

Higher Allerford

Selworthy Farm

⑦

Allerford

Selworthy

A39

New Bridge

50

Brandish Street

100

Buddle Hill

To Minehead

West Luccombe

gate

stile

Great Wood

Packhorse Bridge

Map 4.25: Exmoor 2

0 Kilometres	1	2	3	4
0 Miles	1	2		

curving hummock of Bossington Hill. This footpath then enters a wood via a gateway (waymarked). It soon leaves the wood via a stile on the R. From the stile turn L and make for the gateway directly ahead across the field. Go straight across the next field to the gateway. From here keep to the well-maintained field hedge on the R. Leave the field via a stile and go L along the lane. Just beyond the bend is the small towerless medieval Lynch Chapel-of-Ease *(4)*. Go R over Lynch Bridge — the entrance to the Lynch Country House (waymarked: 'Public Bridleway'). Where the lane forks go R uphill passing an unusual barn and a large thatched dwelling on the L. This lane soon becomes an un-surfaced track. At the path junction go L (waymarked 'Bridleway North Hill/Minehead'). Within a few metres, at the next path junction, go R uphill (waymarked: 'Bridleway Selworthy Beacon/North Hill/Minehead'). Go through a gateway and continue on up the hill following a small stream. At a cross-tracks go L (waymarked: 'Hurlstone Point'). This footpath begins by contouring around the hillside through very distinctive woodland. Leave the wood via the gate and continue to contour around the west side of Bossington Hill on a remarkable footpath shelf.

Ignore the footpath that drops down on the L to Bossington. Beyond the woodland margins the path continues to contour round the hillside.

On approaching Hurlstone Point, with Hurlstone Combe on the R, is a cross-paths. Here go straight on for the headland. Retrace your steps down to the cross-paths and turn L up the scree-strewn and steep Hurlstone Combe (Coast Path way-marking). At the top of the combe go straight on (waymarked: 'Coast Path/Minehead'). Just beyond this fingerpost take the L fork. At the next junction go R (waymarked: 'Coast Path North Hill'), i.e., don't take the rugged clifftop path. The land eastwards is prone to landslips. The track soon relatively levels out and offers views south, and to the north to the South Wales coastline. At the next path junction continue straight on along the ridge (Coast Path waymarking) and within 27 yards (25 m), at the next junction, fork L along the track. Keep on this track skirting above an area of 'improved' farmland. This track then leads directly to Selworthy Beacon ahead — ignore all other tracks to this point.

From Selworthy Beacon continue straight on along the ridge. At the road go L continuing in the same direction. Just beyond the bend in the lane, go R along the track waymarked: 'Selworthy/Dunster'. At the next track junction go R (way-marked: 'Selworthy/Dunster'). This bridlepath goes high above Selworthy Combe. At the next junction go R down into the combe (waymarked: 'Selworthy') — a small memorial hut is seen dead ahead. The track soon drops into woodland with a stream on the R. On approaching Selworthy church *(5)*, go through a gate and then go L up a small flight of stone steps, then over the stile to enter the churchyard.

From the churchyard go R down the lane, passing the War Memorial Cross. Continue on down the hill, passing several thatched estate cottages on the R and, at the next junction, go R along what begins as a metalled lane through a farmyard (way-marked: 'Allerford/No Motor Vehicles'). This green lane can be muddy in places and continues to Allerford. On reaching the surfaced lane continue straight on ignoring the turning on the L. At Allerford village go over the river via the narrow cobbled fourteenth- to fifteenth-century packhorse bridge. Go straight on to the main road. Here go R – proceed with care as this busy main road has no pavement. Follow this road for about 275 yards (250 m) and then go down the green lane on the L. This green lane can also be quite muddy. At the next track junction go straight on (waymarked 'West Luccombe'). Where the track bends sharply to the R take the footpath waymarked: 'West Luccombe' on the L via the stile. Follow the R field boundaries up. This deviation avoids a bad stretch of bridlepath. At the river go over the stile and cross the footbridge ahead. At the lane turn L and follow the road back to Horner and the National Trust car-park.

Horner Water.

1 *Dunkery Beacon*

The summit cairn on Dunkery Beacon, 1705 ft (519 m) above sea level, was erected in September 1935. The Automobile Association's distance viewfinder guides the eye over a huge panorama. Alfred Vowles, writing in 1939, declared that eleven counties (before re-organization) were visible from the summit. Views extend to Porthcawl 22 miles (35.4 km) to the north, Sugar Loaf Mountain (52 miles, 83.6 km); the islands of Flat Holm and Steep Holm; the Malvern Hills and the Forest of Dean, the Vale of Gloucester and the south Cotswolds; the Mendips, the Quantock Hills, the Blackdown Hills, mid-Devon, Dartmoor; and east Cornwall — including Brown Willy and Rough Tor on Bodmin Moor. It also takes in the Horner valley, the Vale of Porlock and Selworthy.

Beacons were lit here in times of emergency, and in recent times for commemorative purposes including the 400th anniversary of the Armada in 1988.

2 *Stoke Pero Church*

Culbone, Oare and Stoke Pero
Three such places you'll seldom here O.

So goes a local rhyme. The medieval Stoke Pero Church was restored in 1897–8 through the generosity of Sir Thomas Acland. The donkey 'Zulu' earned fame by plodding twice a day for many months bringing timber for the roof from Porlock — his portrait hangs in the church.

Opposite: Stoke Pero church.

3   *Horner Wood*

Horner Wood is an ancient oakwood, traditionally unenclosed allowing sheep and wild red deer to roam freely between the moor and its cover. All the wood is a Grade 1 Site of Special Scientific Interest due to its unique biological value. Some 320 species of lichen grow on the oak and ash trees. Dippers can be seen along the length of the river, and pied flycatchers and wood warblers are common nesting birds. The wood is an important wintering area for the Exmoor red deer, which form one of the three largest concentrations of red deer in England.

4   *Lynch Chapel-of-Ease*

The east window in the Lynch Chapel-of-Ease depicts briefly the history of the Manor of Bossington. The manor formed part of the possessions of the abbey of Athelney from about 900 until the Dissolution of the monasteries in the sixteenth century. The abbey was founded by King Alfred the Great in gratitude for his victory over the Danes at Edington in 878 — the Seal of the Abbey and the Arms of the King are shown in the window. The other coats-of-arms are those of the principal holders of the Manor. It eventually passed, through marriage, to Sir Thomas Acland, in 1744.

5   *Selworthy Church*

The parish church of All Saints, Selworthy, is the only one in the district that is still periodically coated with a mixture of lime and tallow to protect the stonework from the effects of the weather. The village here was built in 1828 as a commune for elderly estate retainers. Blaise Hamlet, on the outskirts of Bristol, was the inspiration behind the location of the thatched cottages around a green.

The view south to Dunkery Beacon has been described as one of the most compelling in England and includes most of the National Trust's Holnicote (pronounced 'Hunnicot') Estate, which extends for 12,443 acres (5036 ha). This part of Somerset was given to the National Trust in 1944 by Sir Thomas Acland, the 15th Baronet, to whose family it had belonged for 200 years. Some of the moorland came into Trust ownership in the 1930s.

149

4·26

SOUTH DORSET

THE ISLE OF PURBECK: SWANAGE – KIMMERIDGE – CORFE

STARTING AND FINISHING POINT

Near Swanage Pier, park in large fee-paying car-park (195–035786). This can be a busy town in the holiday season. For this reason, and because of the length of the walk, park early in the morning.

MAP

OS Outdoor Leisure Map 1 : 25 000 Sheet No.15 The Isle of Purbeck.

LENGTH

26 miles (41.8 km)

ASCENT

Some demanding coastal walking: climbs include — $\frac{1}{2}$ mile (0.8 km) out of combe leading on to Emmetts Hill — 250 ft (122 m) — also very steep descent into combe; $\frac{3}{4}$ mile (1.2 km) from Chapman's Pool to Houns-tout Cliff summit — 475 feet (145 m); inland: 350 m Kimmeridge church to road — 125 ft (38 m); $1\frac{1}{4}$ miles (2 km) Whiteway farm to Ridgeway Hill — 305 ft (93 m); $1\frac{1}{4}$ miles (2 km) Challow farm to Rollington Hill — 150 ft (46 m); approx. $\frac{1}{2}$ mile (0.8 km) up to Obelisk on Ballard Down — 275 ft (84 m).

'If one wanted to show a foreigner England, perhaps the wisest course would be to take him to the final section of the Purbeck Hills, and stand him on their summit, a few miles to the east of Corfe'. So wrote E. M. Forster in *Howard's End*.

The Isle of Purbeck is bounded to the north by the River Frome, and by the sea to the south and east. Purbeck's distinctiveness and diversity makes it ideal walking country. This is a challenging walk that explores Purbeck's coastline for $15\frac{1}{2}$ miles (25 km) and the ridge of the Purbeck Hills for $7\frac{3}{4}$ miles (12.5 km), and includes the ruins of Corfe Castle.

An overnight stop is recommended if the day length is short, or use the Ordnance Survey Outdoor Leisure Map (1:25 000) Sheet No 15 'The Isle of Purbeck' to allow taking one of the many shorter return routes that are possible for this walk. This map is an invaluable aid for any walker.

ROUTE DESCRIPTION (Map 4.26)

From the car-park at Swanage *(1)* take the grass track leading over the grassed area to Peveril Point. Continue southwards along the cliff-top path and, at the road, follow Coastal Path signs (waymarked Victorian Trail by a silhouette logo) for a short distance to pick up the trail in Durlston Country Park. A notice here warns of the danger of sea and cliffs. The track here, known as the Isle of Wight Road, leads to Durlston Head.

Follow the track down to the L of Dunster Head Castle (acorn waymarked 'Coast Path'). Continue on the Coast Path over the limestone cliffs towards the lighthouse *(2)*. On approaching Anvil Point, you pass the Tilly Whim Caves entrance on the R. Opposite this point, from a small viewing-platform, you can see on a sea-cliff ledge an inscribed boulder 'Look Round and Read Great Nature's Open Book'. Beyond Anvil Point lighthouse, built in the 1880s, is a stretch of unfenced cliff path which gives good views of Tilly Whim Caves. In the early spring this is a good stretch of coastline for early spider orchids.

The Coast Path enters a field. Here, keep to fence/wall line (L) to avoid unfenced cliff walking. The path then leaves the enclosures via a wooden stile. You soon enter National Trust land at Belle Vue; keep the wire fence to the L. Leaving the National Trust property the route re-enters a field with two small telecommunication towers. Keep to the obvious coastal path on this remote stretch of coastline.

A small detour to Dancing Ledge can be gained via a stile. Dancing Ledge is so-called because the strata here pushes out at a low angle into the sea, causing the water to dance around the rocks. Entering the next National Trust estate, the Coast Path offers extensive views of Seacombe Cliff and the contour strip lynchets on East and West Man — once the medieval open field system of the manor of Worth Matravers. The quarrying works at Seacombe (National Trust) are dangerous (keep outside the fenced areas), but a detour to the ledges is well worth making.

From the quarries follow the track for about 100 yards (metres) and then go L to follow the Coast Path (waymarked 'Winspit 3/4'). The route leaves the National Trust estate, and passes the strip lynchets of East Man (R). This section of the Coast Path is unfenced and care should be taken. The huge amphitheatre of Winspit, with its quarries and ruined buildings, is soon reached and deserves exploring. These cliff quarries were last worked during World War II. Follow the track for a short distance and take the coast path (L) striking above the quarries, and pass West Man. Approaching St Aldhelm's (St Alban's) Head the route enters a quarry high on the cliff and leaves via a flight of steps. The twelfth century St Aldhelm's Chapel is next reached and should be visited *(3)*. The Coast Path then skirts St Aldhelm's Head and from here is a superb stretch of Heritage Coast with views over Chapman's Pool, Houns-tout Cliff, the Kimmeridge Ledges, Broad Bench and beyond.

A natural death, Kimmeridge Bay.

Continue on the well-defined path towards Hill Bottom, passing the Royal Marines' Memorial picnic table (R). At the next footpath junction bear L to head down towards the boathouse (you will come across a short footpath diversion). About 100 yards (metres) before the boathouse take the small path on the R (stone waymark: 'Kimmeridge $3\frac{3}{4}$ coast path'). Drop down to the valley bottom, and cross over a stile, at a footbridge over a stream.

The route follows the steep path making its way over the limestone cap and clay undercliff of Houns-tout Cliff, a distinctive peak capped with limestone. Loose surfaces here, even in dry weather, can be slippery. On the summit ahead are views across to Portland Bill. The Coast Path drops down and passes through a wooden enclave (the Gwyle) with Egmont Bight

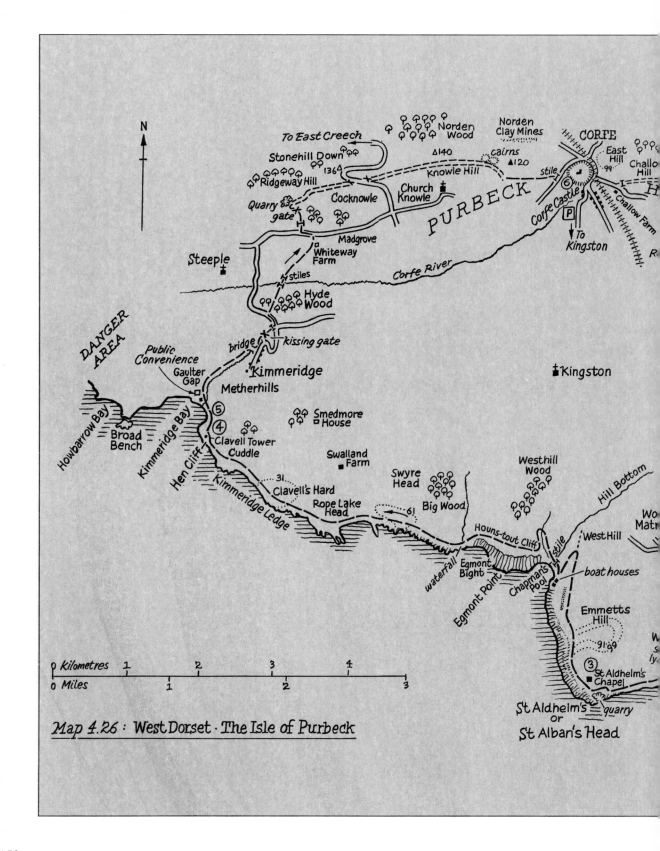

N

To East Creek

Norden
Wood

Norden
Clay Mines

CORFE

East
Hill
99

Challo
Hill

Stonehill Down
1364

Ridgeway Hill

Knowle Hill

Δ140

cairns

Δ120

stile

6

Quarry
gate

Cocknowle

Church
Knowle

PURBECK

Corfe Castle

Challow
Farm

P

To
Kingston

R

Madgrove

Steeple

Whiteway
Farm

Corfe River

stiles

Hyde
Wood

DANGER
AREA

bridge

kissing gate

Kingston

Public
Convenience

Gaulter
Gap

Kimmeridge

Metherhills

Howbarrow Bay

5

4

Smedmore
House

Broad
Bench

Clavell Tower
Cuddle

Kimmeridge Bay

Hen Cliff

Swalland
Farm

Westhill
Wood

Hill Bottom

31

Kimmeridge Ledge

Clavell's Hard

Rope Lake
Head

Swyre
Head

Big Wood

Wo
Matr

61

Hours-tout Cliff

stile

West Hill

Wo
sly

waterfall

Egmont
Bight

boat houses

Egmont Point

Chapmans
Pool

Emmetts
Hill

91·99

W
sly

3

St Aldhelm's
Chapel

0 Kilometres 1 2 3 4

0 Miles 1 2 3

St Aldhelm's
or
St Alban's Head

quarry

Map 4.26 : West Dorset · The Isle of Purbeck

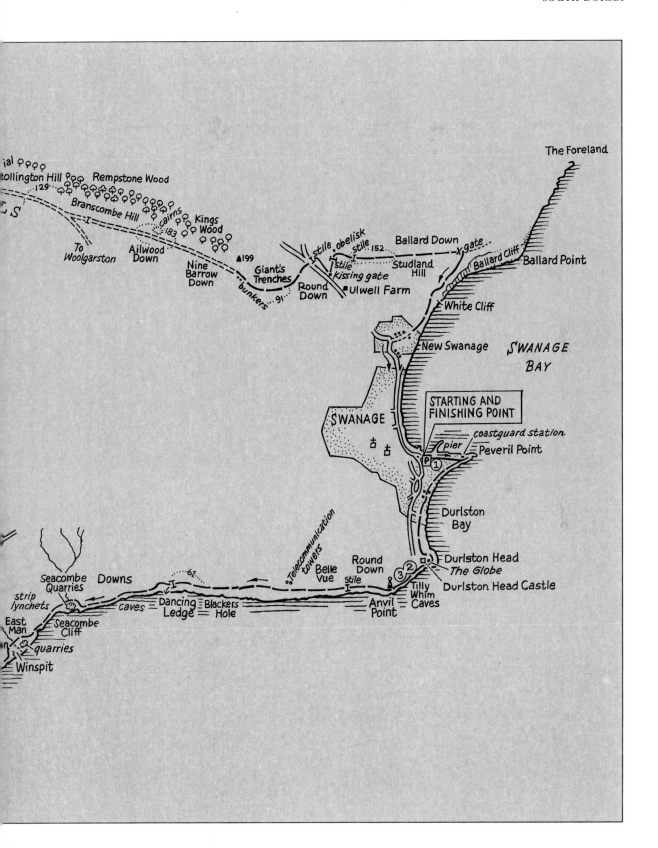

The Foreland

ial
tollington Hill
129
Rempstone Wood
Branscombe Hill
cairns
Kings
Wood
183
To
Woolgarston
Ailwood
Down
Nine
Barrow
Down
▲199
Giant's
Trenches
bunkers
91
Round
Down
stile
obelisk
stile 152
Ballard Down
x gate
Ballard Cliff
Ballard Point
stile
kissing gate
Ulwell Farm
Studland
Hill
White Cliff

New Swanage

SWANAGE
BAY

STARTING AND
FINISHING POINT

SWANAGE

coastguard station

pier
Peveril Point

P
①

Durlston
Bay

Telecommunication
towers

Belle
Vue

Round
Down
stile

Durlston Head
The Globe
Durlston Head Castle

Seacombe
Quarries
Downs
67
③②
Tilly
Whim
Caves

strip
lynchets

caves
Dancing
Ledge
Blackers
Hole
Anvil
Point

East
Man
Seacombe
Cliff
quarries

Winspit

waterfall on the L. Continue on the Coast Path over Rope Lake Head and Clavell's Hard, above the Kimmeridge Ledges. 'Hard' refers to a natural place where boats could land, or a quay. Approaching Clavel Tower (L) you may notice small sections of rail — the railway used to take shale down to a quay below Clavel Tower. Clavel Tower now suffers a little behind barbed wire *(4)*.

The shale and clay cliffs of Kimmeridge Bay lie within the Smedmore Estate. At the boathouses at Kimmeridge Bay *(5)* is an information centre run by the Dorset Trust for Nature Conservation. Follow the Coast Path round to the public conveniences. Here follow the private road for about 55 yards (50 m) and go along the footpath (R) waymarked 'Kimmeridge $\frac{3}{4}$ Steeple $1\frac{1}{2}$'. The walk now leaves the coastline and takes an inland route to head back over the Purbeck Hills.

Keep the field boundary on the R and, at the next footpath junction, bear R (yellow waymark) over the footbridge to the village of Kimmeridge. At the road, turn L and follow the street up. The parish church of St Nicholas is mostly nineteenth-century, but its Norman south doorway still remains. Go through the churchyard. The churchyard path passes 'the Old Parsonage' (R). Negotiate the kissing-gate and head straight up the field.

On reaching the road, cross the stile, turn L and follow the road for abut 190 yards (175 m) and take the next footpath on the R. Keep Hyde Wood on your R and continue straight down to the bottom of the field. Pass through the metal gate, and you can see Corfe Castle ahead. Bear half-L for a wooden stile in the field perimeter. On approaching this stile, the sixteenth-century tower of Steeple Church can be seen to the L.

Go over the next stile, through a small copse and leave by another stile. Cross the next field, go over another stile and continue on the same line heading for the R side of the copse ahead. Here, walk up the edge of the copse for about 27 yards (25 m), to find the small clearing leading into the next field. Crops may be growing here. Your legal right is straight across on the public right-of-way, but commonsense will bring you to Whiteway Farm ahead. At the farm, follow the farm track (L) — yellow waymarker. Turn L at the road and within a short distance go up the track on the R. Where this track turns to the R (private) continue straight on over a wooden stile (waymarked). At the top end of the field go through the gate and bear L following the bridlepath up on to Ridgeway Hill, a part of the Purbeck Hills.

Disused Purbeck Stone quarry, Winspit.

On reaching the summit bear R along the well-defined track (waymarked: 'Cocknowle $\frac{1}{2}$ and Corfe $2\frac{1}{4}$'). Proceeding eastwards from the ridgeway to the north (L), you can see Purbeck Forest, Brownsea Island, Poole and Studland Heath. The ridge path emerges on to a road, and here to the L are some interesting examples of stone-made graffiti on the hillslope.

At the road go through the metal gate and continue straight on for 27 yards (25 m) and go through the next gate ahead to pick up the ridge route on Knowle Hill (waymarked 'Bridleway Corfe Castle $1\frac{3}{4}$ ml'). The ridge path passes several hill-top tumuli. Soon after, the track begins to drop down along the south side of West Hill to Corfe Castle. Stay on the bridlepath, with the castle and Corfe church in view, and ignore the footpath leading off from the R.

At the next road, cross over the stile. Turn L and after crossing a small bridge follow the footpath immediately on the R, which skirts round the outer walls of the castle *(6)*.

From the market square, with your back to the National Trust shop, walk straight on and bear L passing the Greyhound, an old coaching inn. Cross the road before the bridge to avoid a dangerous blind bend and take the next lane on the R (Sandy Hill), passing under a disused railway bridge.

At Challow Farm go L along the bridleway (waymarked: 'Ulwell $3\frac{1}{2}$'). At the next footpath junction go L (waymarked: 'Bridlepath Rollington Hill $\frac{1}{2}$ and Ulwell $3\frac{1}{2}$'). Near the radio aerial on Rollington Hill go through the L gate at the path junction (waymarked: 'Ridge path Ulwell $2\frac{3}{4}$'), ignoring R gate to Little Woolgarston. Continue along the ridge path, which offers views back to Corfe Castle and the valley of the River Corfe, and over Studland Heath.

You next enter the National Trust Ailwood Down estate. At the top of the hill take the R track (waymarked: 'NT Swanage and Studland bridlepath') and pass a group of prehistoric ridge-top barrows. At the far end of the National Trust property go through the gate. Continue on the ridge path (waymarked 'Ulwell $1\frac{1}{4}$') at the next path junction, ignoring the path to Knitson. The OS obelisk at the end of Nine Barrow Down marks the highest point on the ridge and Purbeck — 650 ft (198 m) above sea level. At the war bunkers skirt round the R side of Nine Barrow Down, and the bridlepath you are following drops down to enter the National Trust property of Godlingston Hill. Where the track next divides skirt L of Round Down to meet the Studland Road, passing the deep Giant's Trenches. At the road go L and at the next road junction ('Corfe Castle/Studland') cross the road and enter the National Trust estate of Ballard Down. Go over the stile and bear R along the footpath at the bottom of the

Corfe Castle from Challow Farm.

wood (do not take the paddock path). Go through the kissing-gate and bear L up the path waymarked 'The Obelisk' — the last steep climb of the walk. At the top of the hill cross the stile for the Obelisk. This originally stood outside the church of St Mary Woolnoth in London. Bear R along the enclosed (wire fencing) ridge path and ignore the path to Studland. Continue over Ballard Down/Studland Hill — the ridge was on a smuggling route from Swanage Bay towards Corfe. As you approach the end of the chalk ridge the Isle of Wight can be seen. On reaching a gate at Ballard Cliff, the path cuts down three-quarters-R to join the Coast Path after crossing a stile, and following the edge of the field. The Coast Path returns to Swanage via White Cliff (National Trust).

On reaching Swanage suburbia, by the bungalows (R), follow the footpath (waymarked) away from the cliff edge. At the road turn L. Follow the occasional footpath signs on the roadside through the private estate of Ballard. On reaching the public road (Ballard Way), continue straight on, bear L at the post office and continue on the main road back to Swanage sea front and the pier car-park.

1   *Swanage*

Until the mid-nineteenth century, business in Swanage was dominated by the quarrying and exporting of Purbeck Stone and Purbeck Marble from the cliffs to the south and west. On the quay are the remains of rail-lines used to transport the stone to jetties. Here it was loaded onto barges and shipped to London. John Mowlem and his nephew George Burt, local quarry contractors, made much money shipping stone, and their barges returned with London stonework salvaged from demolished buildings. This stone was incorporated into the many Victorian structures in the town — the town hall includes the carved mid-seventeenth century entrance of the Mercers' Hall, Cheapside. The coming of the railway in 1885 saw the rapid development of the town as a seaside resort.

2   *Local birdlife*

Many birds, such as waders, skuas and shearwaters, are seen during migration times as they fly over the Channel coast, heading east in spring and west in autumn. Terns and gannets may be seen throughout the summer, usually feeding off-shore. Geese and divers fly past in winter months, generally en route to and from local feeding grounds. Look out for Arctic tern, occasionally seen during April–May, and the Great Northern diver in December and January.

3   *St Aldhelm's Chapel*

On a windswept headland, some 354 ft (108 m) above the sea, sits the chapel of St Aldhelm, which takes its name from the first Bishop of Sherborne, AD 705. This square chapel — unusual for a religious building — contains beautiful vaulting in its twelfth-century roof, which springs from a central column. It is believed that the chapel was originally a chantry, where a priest would perform masses for the safety of sailors. The chapel had no parochial status and during the eighteenth century it was described as ruinous. The isolated ruin had come to be regarded as a place of superstition — 'The Devil's Chapel'. Extensive repairs were carried out in the fourteenth century and the cross was erected on the turret in 1873.

4   *Clavel Tower*

Clavel Tower, on the cliff overlooking Kimmeridge Bay, is a folly built by the Reverend John Richards, who assumed the name of Clavel(l) upon inheriting the nearby Smedmore estate. The three-storey circular tower was built in 1831 and is surrounded by a colonnade. Though not built as a look-out, it was used by the coastguard in the mid-nineteenth century.

5   *Kimmeridge Bay*

Kimmeridge Clay was laid down some 150 million years ago and contains several thin layers of bituminous shale known as 'Kimmeridge Coal', or 'Blackstone'. From the Iron Age to Roman times this shale was used to make armlets and rings. During the eighteenth century this was further exploited, first in the production of alum (a chemical used in the dyeing, printing and tanning industries), then it was used as a fuel in a glassmaking works. The initial optimism in the latter venture led to the construction of a large jetty which was subsequently damaged in storms.

Kimmeridge Bay lies within the Purbeck Marine Wildlife Reserve, sponsored by the Dorset Trust for Nature Conservation. Kimmeridge Ledges provide excellent shore habitats for various types of wildlife. A double low tide gives more light for a longer period of time, which is one of the reasons why seaweeds are so abundant and varied. Above the high water mark can be found small and rough periwinkles and channelled wrack, and below this mark grow spiral, knotted and bladder wracks, and beadlet anemones have a strong foothold. Below the low-water mark grows kelp, podweed, red seaweeds and ross coral, while brittlestars and rock lobsters crawl over the seabed.

6   *Corfe Castle*

The word 'corfe' is derived from the Anglo-Saxon and means a 'cutting, gap or pass', aptly describing the physical situation of the settlement on the Purbeck Hills. There was a royal castle at Corfe in William the Conqueror's time, although much of what remains today is due to subsequent development. The keep was built in the time of Henry I and most of the defences of the outer bailey were constructed during the reigns of King John and Edward I. The castle's ruined state is attributable to the Parliamentarian engineers who were ordered to destroy it in 1646 following the surrender of the Royalist garrison after a long siege.

The Old Hall sits on the site of a much older residence. It is possible that this was the home of Elfrida, stepmother of King Edward the Martyr. It is believed that she plotted to depose Edward in favour of her own son, Ethelred the Unready. Tradition has it that in 978, Edward was killed by Elfrida at the castle. He soon became venerated as a saint and martyr.

DEVON

DARTMOOR: A SOUTH TO NORTH TRAVERSE

STARTING POINT
Small car-park at Harford Moor
Gate, south Dartmoor, about 1
mile (1.6 km) east of the village of
Harford, 2.5 miles (4 km) north
of Ivybridge.
FINISHING POINT
Belstone village, north Dartmoor.
MAP
OS 1 : 25 000 Outdoor Leisure
'Dartmoor'.
LENGTH
27 miles (43.5 km)
ASCENT
7 climbs — $1\frac{1}{4}$ miles (2 km),
ascent 413 ft (126 m) from
Harford Moor Gate to Piles Hill;
$\frac{1}{3}$ mile (0.5 km), ascent 144 ft
(44 m) to Three Barrows; $\frac{1}{3}$ mile
(0.5 km), ascent 207 ft (63 m) to
Bellever Tor; 0.6 mile (1 km),
ascent 215 ft (65 m) to East Dart
Waterfall; $\frac{1}{3}$ mile (0.5 km), ascent
128 ft (39 m) to Statts House;
$\frac{1}{3}$ mile (0.5 km), ascent 164 ft
(50 m) to Quintin's Man; 1 mile
(1.6 km), ascent 170 ft (52 m) to
summit of Whitehorse Hill.

This challenging walk traverses some of Dartmoor's wildest terrain, taking in the individually distinctive south and north moorland plateau areas of the National Park. It should not be attempted in poor weather. The northern portion of the walk, from Winney's Down to Knattaborough lies within the Okehampton Firing Range — firing times must be checked before setting out. Use the telephone answering service on Okehampton (0837) 52939.

ROUTE DESCRIPTION (Map 4.27)

From Harford Moor Gate go north uphill keeping the enclosure wall on your L. Where this wall swings down to the L continue straight on over the brow of the hill. With Sharp Tor well in view bear quarter-R up onto Piles Hill continuing in the direction of Sharp Tor. Piles Copse — a primeval oak wood — is seen deep in the Erme valley; away to the L are the clay tips of Lee Moor.

Pass several prehistoric cairns on your R and you soon reach the trackbed of the Redlake Tramway. Stay on this track northwards passing Sharp Tor (L), noticing its large prehistoric summit cairn.

Just beyond Sharp Tor leave the trackbed and follow the broad path up to the summit of Three Barrows. An OS obelisk stands at 1522 ft (464 m) above sea level. Three large prehistoric cairns crown the summit. From the obelisk strike quarter-L across the moor. Head for Leftlake Mires and the small china-clay waste tips that soon come into view *(1)*.

Continue northwards along the tramway, which contours round Quickbeam Hill giving good views over the upper reaches of the River Erme. Within $1\frac{3}{4}$ miles (2.8 km) from Leftlake a series of low ruined structures can be seen on the R. Here, leave the tramway and follow these former clay settling pits round to Crossways. Standing incongruously in the flat plain of Red Lake Mire is a much larger china-clay tip, which has a volcano-like appearance.

Pick up the tramway again and head straight for the waste tip and the flooded clay pits. The terminal of the tramway is soon reached. Skirt round the east (R) flank of the clay tip and then head due north for Fishlake Mire — this is an almost featureless landscape, but make for the low coll between Naker's Hill and Ryder's Hill. Boggy ground and long moorland grasses make for some arduous walking ahead over this wild terrain.

Despite the hostile environment, a large number of tinners worked in the area, especially from about 400 to 600 years ago. The low walls of a tinner's hut are passed on the L. From the tinner's hut cross the small stream rising from Fishlake Mire which, up to the end of the eighteenth century, was known as Hunavill's Bed. Keep the infant River Avon on your R, the valley of which bears many tinners' spoil heaps, and continue northwards over the higher ground on the east side of Naker's Hill. Staying on the higher ground avoids Aune (Anon) Head Mires — a notorious area of bad ground.

Continue over the brow of Skir Hill. A long prominent tinners' gert (Skir Gut) comes into view. Keep this ancient working on your R and head straight across the moor over east Ter Hill and across Down Ridge.

Heading over Down Ridge make for the stroll — a tongue of moorland that drops down between the moorland enclosures above Hexworthy. Go through the moorgate to leave the south moor. The next stretch of walking involves crossing Dartmoor's central farmbelt. Go down the track, cross the lane and continue straight on down the track passing a bungalow on your L and several superbly thatched cottages. At the farmyard bear L through the gateway and stay on the public footpath (waymarked) — this can be a muddy spot. Leave the farmyard via the gate and follow the bottom of the field. Enter the next field (waymarked) and keep the well-built granite wall on your L. Ahead can be seen Combestone Tor and the West Dart River. Cross into the next field via the stone stiles and follow the yellow markers to Hexworthy (Huccaby) Bridge. Cross the narrow medieval structure and stay on the lane passing Huccaby Farm. At the main Dartmeet to Princetown road go L and follow the roadside path to the slate-clad Huccaby Cottage. Soon after go R, through the gateway, and head up to Huccaby Tor passing the low earth remains of Huccaby Ring.

From Huccaby Tor continue on the same line and leave the newtake (moorland enclosure) via a stile. Stay on the broad track that leads towards Bellever Tor and Laughter Tor — a solitary prehistoric menhir (standing stone) known as Laughter Man is seen on the skyline ahead. The route passes several nineteenth-century tin-mine shafts. A much-robbed prehistoric double stone

Bellever.

row leads off from the menhir. From the standing stone, which is some 8 ft 7 ins (2.6 m) high, take the R fork up to Laughter Tor. A large ruined pound is passed on the L — moormen used to speak of this as the 'sheep measure'. From Laughter Tor — 1378 ft (420 m) above sea level — continue straight for the massive Bellever Tor keeping to the L of the outer parts of Bellever Forest. At the time of writing, storm damage and clear-felling operations have taken their toll.

From the summit of Bellever Tor — 1453 ft (443 m) above sea level — the views are extensive. Drop down the rough side of the tor and continue over Lakehead Hill to Postbridge via Kraps Ring — a prehistoric settlement.

At the main Moretonhampstead — Two Bridges road go R and pass the post office and village store (L), and go over the road bridge that runs parallel to the medieval clapper bridge *(2)*. Turn L immediately after the bridge through a hunting gate. Pass through this field following the wall (R) towards Ringhill, then turn L and follow the wall to the river, passing Hartyland (R). Go through a hunting gate here and turn R. Stay on the river-side bridle path up the East Dart River, passing through another two hunting gates in the small plantation near Hartyland.

On entering Hartland Tor Newtake, the path runs straight up the East Dart valley close to the river bank passing below Hartland Tor. The south-to-north route begins to penetrate the north Dartmoor plateau. Cross the stile over the stone wall at the far side of the newtake to enter the extensive Stannon Tor Newtake. Continue on near the river until a tributary stream (Lade Hill Bottom) flows in from the north (R) near to where the East Dart River swings abruptly to the L. On the opposite side of the river you can see a take-off point for a leat which ran to Powder Mills, a nineteenth-century gunpowder factory. Cross over the stream near to where it enters the East Dart River above a weir. Continue on in the same direction following a path uphill which, in its turn, soon veers to the L, and follow the East Dart upstream. Go through the gate and, staying on the path, cross Winney's Down Brook. Follow a path round the L side of the hill to reach the base of the East Dart Waterfall. The fall occurs diagonally across the riverbed, which the water has deeply incised.

Staying on the river's L bank (i.e., keep the river on the L) continue up the valley to the narrow defile of Sandy Hole Pass passing extensive tin-streaming spoils on the L. Keep on the path running over the top of Sandy Hole Pass *(3)*. Here the valley opens out into Broad Marsh. Continue straight on the path that runs above the flood plain, and follow this path, which eventually skirts round half-R to avoid boggy ground. The path soon becomes poorly-defined through the luxuriant grass growth;

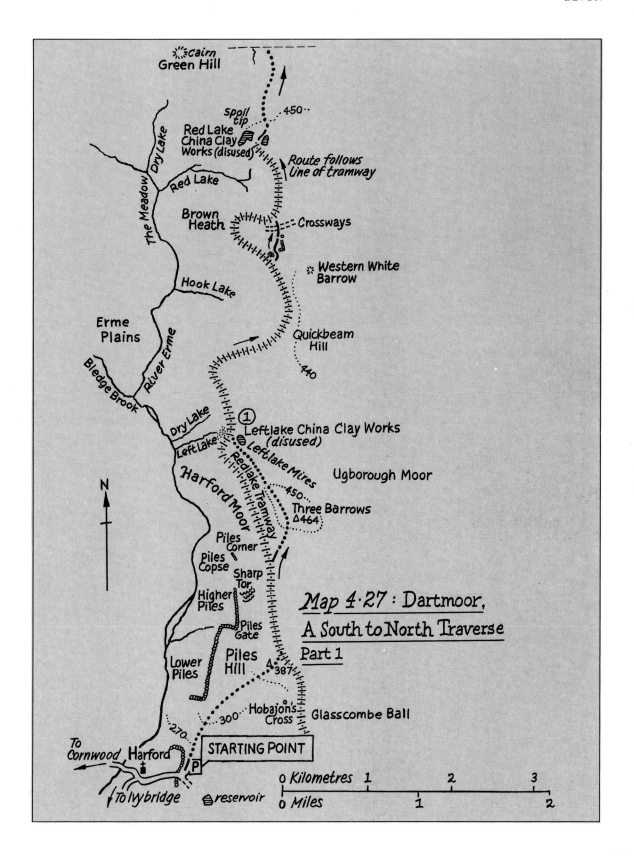

Map 4·27 : Dartmoor,
A South to North Traverse
Part 1

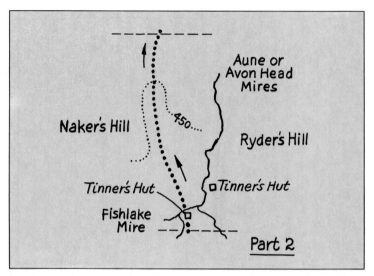

head straight on in the direction of a shallow combe and on approaching it turn R uphill to follow the peat pass to Statts House, a ruined eighteenth-century peat-cutter's house, on Winney's Down (Marsh Hill), some 1768 ft (520 m) above sea level.

Continue along the crest of the Down (northwards) in the direction of Quintin's Man — which comprises stable and look-out hut and summit cairn — passing the remains of another peat-cutter's home on the L. Drop down into the infant valley of the South Teign River and, keeping the range poles and notice board on your L, cross the river and continue on up the slope following the range poles. Okehampton Firing Range is on the L. From the look-out hut on Quintin's Man continue straight on along a military track that runs north-north-east and keep the range poles here well to the R. You are now in the Okehampton Range. On Whitehorse Hill summit the military track is granite-paved and it swings away to the R through a peat pass; keep on this track for about 260 yards (237 m) and then bear L to contour around to the lowly tor on Hangingstone Hill. The flat area between Whitehorse and Hangingstone Hill is extremely boggy and should be avoided.

From Hangingstone Hill continue northwards, along the well-defined military track, in the direction of Steeperton Tor — the views across this northern fastness contrast markedly with those encountered on the south moor. Steeperton Tor has unusually severe slopes for moorland Dartmoor and it rises mountain-like above the waters of the Steeperton Brook on the one side and the River Taw on the other. The track drops down into Steeperton Gorge — a narrow defile for the young River Taw and haunt of ring ouzels. Cross the river via the ford and then go L upstream for about 150 yards (137 m) to the remains of Knack Mine — a

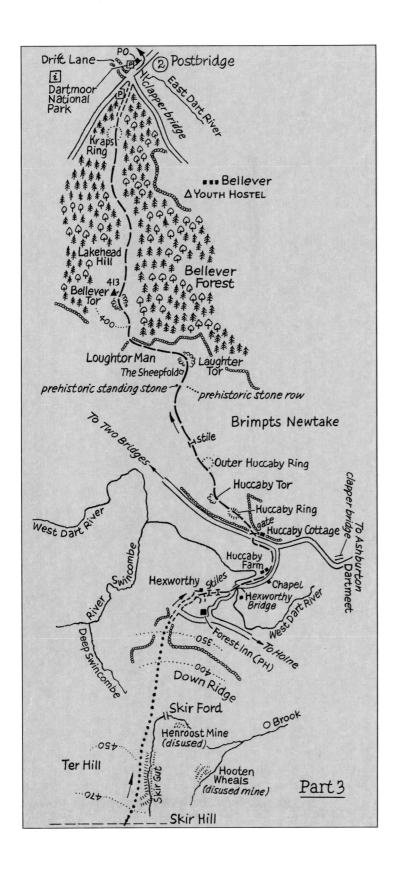

Drift Lane

PO

② Postbridge

i
Dartmoor
National
Park

Clapper bridge

East Dart River

Kraps
Ring

■■■ Bellever
△ Youth Hostel

Lakehead
Hill

Bellever
Forest

413
Bellever
Tor

400

Loughtor Man
The Sheepfold

Laughter
Tor

prehistoric standing stone ········· prehistoric stone row

Brimpts Newtake

To Two Bridges

stile

Outer Huccaby Ring

Huccaby Tor

West Dart River

Huccaby Ring

gate
Huccaby Cottage

To Ashburton
Dartmeet

Clapper bridge

River Swincombe

Huccaby
Farm

Hexworthy   stiles
I-I

Chapel

Hexworthy
Bridge

West Dart River

Forest Inn (PH)

To Holne

Deep Swincombe

350

400

Down Ridge

Skir Ford

O Brook

Henroost Mine
(disused)

450

Ter Hill

Skir Gut

Hooten
Wheals
(disused mine)

Part 3

470

Skir Hill

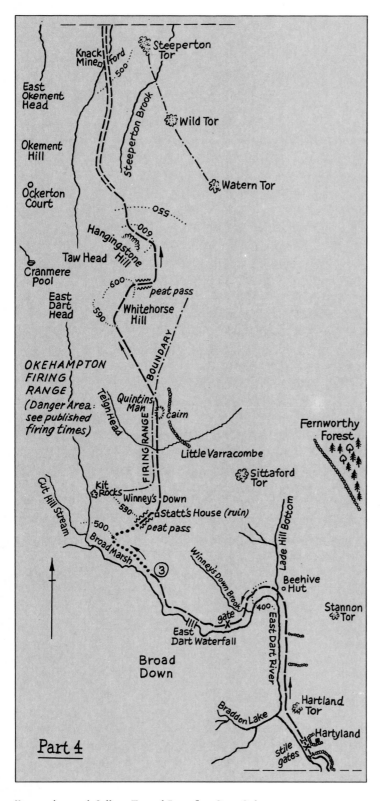

East Okement Head

Knack Mine Ford

Steeperton Tor

500

Okement Hill

Steeperton Brook

Wild Tor

Ockerton Court

Watern Tor

Taw Head

Hangingstone Hill

oss

600

Cranmere Pool

East Dart Head

590

600

peat pass

Whitehorse Hill

OKEHAMPTON FIRING RANGE

(Danger Area: see published firing times)

BOUNDARY

Teign Head

Quintins Man

cairn

FIRING RANGE

Little Varracombe

Fernworthy Forest

Sittaford Tor

Kit Rocks

Winney's Down

590

Statt's House (ruin)

peat pass

Cut Hill Stream

500

Broad Marsh

③

Winney's Down Brook

Lade Hill Bottom

Beehive Hut

Stannon Tor

gate

400

East Dart Waterfall

East Dart River

Broad Down

Braddon Lake

Hartland Tor

Hartyland

stile gates

Part 4

View north towards Bellever Tor and Forest from Down Ridge.

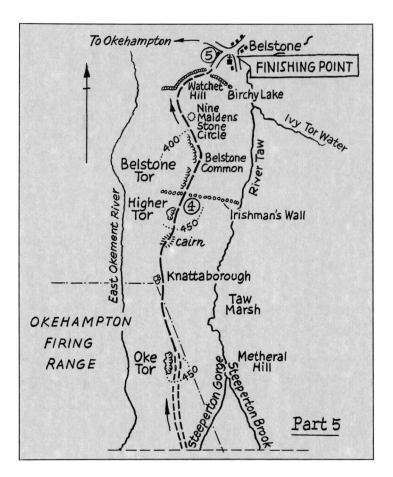

small nineteenth-century tin venture. Retrace your steps to the ford and continue along the track uphill. The military look-out and stable huts on Oke Tor are soon reached.

Continue on the grass track northwards from Oke Tor along the ridge ahead, passing the next, smaller, outcrop known as Knattaborough. At this point you leave the Okehampton Firing Range. Continue northwards for Belstone Tors, passing a small, grass-covered prehistoric cairn, to reach Higher Tor. Here rowan, bilberry and tenuous moorland grasses have a foothold in the granite. Cross the Irishman's Wall (4) and continue along the ridge crest to Belstone Tor and then drop to Tors End — the northernmost outcrop on Watchet Hill marking the end of the Belstone range of tors. From the summit drop quarter-L down the northern slopes. The Nine Maidens prehistoric retaining circle is soon reached. From here pick up the track that leads to the moorgate at Watchet and keep the stone wall close to the L. Go through the moorgate and continue straight on along the lane passing the Belstone Water Treatment Works (on L). You soon come to the village of Belstone (5) and the end of a remarkable walk.

1   China clay

The remote china-clay deposits at Left Lake and Red Lake Mires were exploited soon after the turn of the twentieth century. The Red Lake Tramway, with a gauge of 3 ft (0.9 m), officially opened on 11 September, 1911. The railway carried people and general freight, while china clay was pumped via a parallel running pipeline to settling pits where micas, the unwanted wastes, settled. Inspection manholes and air ducts still exist along the course of the pipeline. By 1932 the best clay was exhausted and The China Clay Corporation was liquidated in 1933.

2   Postbridge

The village of Postbridge dates from the late eighteenth century, when in 1772 two Acts of Parliament were passed allowing the formation of the Moretonhampstead and Tavistock Turnpike Trusts. These two Trusts contracted a local moorman and his sons to build the new road, which is the basis of the present B3212, and all the bridges along its length. Postbridge offered a natural stopping place half-way

At the East Dart Waterfall.

across the moor and it was only a matter of time before an inn was built and then a post office, shop, chapel and houses. Before the road was built a trans-moorland track already existed and at Postbridge a ford and a medieval clapper bridge crossed the East Dart River.

3   *Sandy Hole Pass*

At Sandy Hole Pass, the river is confined between steep slopes. In Tudor times, tinners had excavated the riverbed here to drain the mire of Broad Marsh and to quicken the flow of the river to carry away tin wastes and sand from their workings. Downstream a great quantity of sand was subsequently deposited on the flood plain below the Hole; much further on, Dartmouth officials soon began to complain of the silting-up of their port due to tinners' activities on Dartmoor.

Richard Strode, Member of Parliament for Plympton, took up the case on behalf of the port and that of Plymouth, which was suffering like problems from tinners in the Meavy and Plym valleys. The promotion of a Bill prohibiting unrestrained digging by tinners got him in trouble with the Stannary Courts. He was presented in his absence before each of the four Stannary Courts and fined a total of £160. On refusing to pay he was thrown into Lydford Castle gaol. Strode managed to have his case brought to Parliament, and a statute granted him and his associates immunity from future interference.

4   *The Irishman's Wall*

The broken-down boundary work of the Irishman's Wall is a lasting testimony to the folly of trying to infringe upon the rights of common. One explanation of the wall's origin concerns a band of Irish Protestants who, driven from Ulster in the eighteenth century, attempted a settlement on this part of Dartmoor; they wanted to create a vast enclosure of moorland for cultivation. The parishioners of Belstone and Okehampton were, understandably, irate and they destroyed the wall as soon as it was finished and drove the immigrants away.

5   *Belstone*

The small village of Belstone is worthy of exploration. The old stocks still stand on the village green and nearby is a small pound in which stray animals were impounded. The village post office, which has a namestone denoting it as the 'Telegraphy Office', was once a Zion Chapel — a datestone of 1841 can be seen above the front door. The church, dedicated to St Mary, dates to the fifteenth century and is famed for its peal of six bells, five of which are eighteenth century.

APPENDICES
Access for the Walker

It is important to realize at the outset that the designation of a National Park, Heritage Coast, Area of Outstanding Natural Beauty, Environmentally Sensitive Area or National Trail does not change the ownership of land within it in any way. In the case of Dartmoor National Park in 1991 only 1.4 per cent of the land was actually owned by the National Park Authority, and only 25 per cent by all 'public' bodies (excluding the Duchy of Cornwall) combined, e.g. Forestry Commission, Ministry of Defence, National Trust and South West Water plc. The laws of access and trespass apply just as much to areas of private land within a designated area as to those outside it.

The National Parks and Access to the Countryside Act of 1949 required County Councils in England and Wales to prepare maps that showed all paths over which the public had a right to walk. The final form of the map is referred to as a Definitive Map and local copies are held at the offices of the County Councils and by Dartmoor and Exmoor National Park Authorities. The inclusion of a public right-of-way on a Definitive Map can be taken as proof that such exists. Paths can only be diverted or deleted from a Definitive Map by the raising of a Diversion Order or an Extinguishment Order respectively. The paths are classified as either footpaths (for walkers only) or bridleways (for walkers, horse riders and cyclists). For definitive routes always use up-to-date maps. Public

rights of way are included on the Ordnance Survey's 1 : 50 000 First and Second Series (i.e. Landranger), the 1 : 25 000 Second Series (i.e. Pathfinder) and the Outdoor Leisure Maps.

On Dartmoor and Exmoor the rights-of-way network extends for some 1000 miles (1609 km) and the Park Authorities are responsible for all matters concerning the network. All these rights-of-way are well waymarked in both National Parks. Public footpaths in Heritage Coast areas are also well waymarked. Elsewhere the situation largely depends on the attitudes of the County Councils and District Councils. In the South West this situation varies enormously — one part of a county may be well waymarked, another area almost neglected.

If this was the end of the matter, the right of access for the walker within the South West peninsula would be severely restricted, since there are considerable areas of land without any public rights-of-way and sometimes the legal paths do not provide logical walking options. Fortunately, however, in practice access to large areas is allowed via a number of mechanisms such as common-land status and access agreement areas. Ownership by a number of bodies, including South West Water, the Forestry Commission and the National Trust, have also increased walking opportunities.

Safety

The routes described in this publication vary considerably in both length and difficulty. Some, at least the easy walks, should with reasonable care be safe at any time of the year and under almost any weather conditions; the more difficult walks on the other hand cross some of the wildest and roughest country in Great Britain and should only be attempted by fit walkers who are properly clothed and equipped and have command of the techniques involved in walking and route finding.

It cannot be too strongly emphasized that weather and conditions can change very rapidly in moorland and coastal areas. The severity of a walk will generally be much greater in the winter. What is a drizzle in a valley could be a blizzard on the moor top. Hot summer days are frequent and also have their hazards — sunburn, heat exhaustion and heat strokes can occur unless walkers are properly prepared. This must be borne in mind when selecting clothing and equipment before a walk.

In coastal areas high winds can make walking slow and tiring. Very high winds can make it particularly dangerous on cliff edges. The coastguards are responsible for dealing with emergencies that occur on the coast or at sea. To contact them dial 999 and ask for the coastguard — the service relies on the public reporting vessels or people that are in distress.

If you meet with an accident, either to one of your party or by discovering someone else injured, give what first aid you are capable of administering. If necessary, shelter the casualty. Write down the grid reference of the incident, and then locate the nearest village or telephone. Ideally two people should go for assistance, leaving someone behind with the casualty, but obviously the decision will be determined by the number in the party.

The golden rules for safety in moorland and mountain areas (and, to a lesser extent, the coastal routes) are:

DO
Carry appropriate clothing and equipment, all of which should be in sound condition.
Carry map and compass and be practised in their use.
Leave a note of your intended route with a responsible person (and keep to it!)
Report your return as soon as possible.
Keep warm, but not overwarm, at all times.
Eat nourishing foods, and rest at regular intervals.
Avoid becoming exhausted.
Know first aid and the correct procedure in case of accidents or illness.
Obtain a weather forecast before you start. You can obtain an inshore weather forecast from Marinecall (0898) 500458, and a regional forecast from Weathercall (0898) 500404.

DO NOT
Go out on your own unless you are very experienced. Three is a good number.
Leave any member of the party behind on remote moorland, unless help has to be summoned.
Explore old mine workings or caves, or climb cliffs (except scrambling ridges).
Attempt routes which are beyond your skill and experience.
A booklet, *Safety on Mountains*, is published by the British Mountaineering Council, Crawford House, Precinct Centre, Booth Street East, Manchester M13 9RZ.

Giving a Grid Reference

Giving a grid reference is an excellent way of 'pinpointing' a feature, such as a church or tor, on an Ordnance Survey map.

Grid lines, which are used for this purpose, are shown on the 1 : 25 000 Outdoor Leisure, 1 : 25 000 Pathfinder and 1 : 50 000 Landranger maps produced by the Ordnance Survey; these are the maps most commonly used by walkers. They are the thin blue lines (1 kilometre apart) running vertically and horizontally across the map, producing a network of small squares. Each line, whether vertical or horizontal, is given a number from 00 to 99, with the sequence repeating itself every 100 lines. The 00 lines are slightly thicker than the others thus producing large squares with sides made up of 100 small squares, thus representing 100 kilometres. Each of these large squares is identified by two letters. The entire network of lines covering the British Isles, excluding Ireland, is called the National Grid.

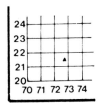 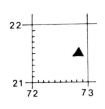

The left-hand diagram above shows a corner of an Ordnance Survey 1 : 50 000 Landranger map which contains a Youth Hostel. Using this map, the method of determining a grid reference is as follows:

Step 1

Holding the map in the normal upright position, note the number of the 'vertical' grid line to the left of the hostel. This is 72.

Step 2

Now imagine that the space between this grid line and the adjacent one to the right of the hostel is divided into ten equal divisions (the diagram on the right does this for you). Estimate the number of these 'tenths' that the hostel lies to the right of the left-hand grid line. This is 8. Add this to the number found in Step 1 to make 728.

Step 3

Note the number of the grid line below the hostel and add it on to the number obtained above. This is 21, so that the number becomes 72821.

Step 4

Repeat Step 2 for the space containing the hostel, but now in a vertical direction. The final number to be added is 5, making 728215. This is called a six-figure grid reference. This, coupled with the number or name of the appropriate Landranger or Outdoor Leisure map, will enable the Youth Hostel to be found.

A full grid reference will also include the identification of the appropriate 100 kilometre square of the National Grid; for example, SD 728215. The information is given in the margin of each map.

Countryside Access Charter

YOUR RIGHTS OF WAY ARE

Public footpaths — on foot only. Sometimes way-marked in yellow.

Bridleways — on foot, horseback and pedal cycle. Sometimes waymarked in blue.

Byways (usually old roads), most 'Roads Used as Public Paths' and, of course, public roads — all traffic.

Use maps, signs and waymarks. Ordnance Survey Pathfinder and Landranger maps show most public rights-of-way.

ON RIGHTS OF WAY YOU CAN

Take a pram, pushchair or wheelchair if practicable.

Take a dog (on a lead or under close control).

Take a short route round an illegal obstruction or remove it sufficiently to get past.

YOU HAVE A RIGHT TO GO FOR RECREATION TO

Public parks and open spaces — on foot.

Most commons near older towns and cities — on foot and sometimes on horseback.

Private land where the owner has a formal agreement with the local authority.

IN ADDITION YOU CAN USE BY LOCAL OR ESTABLISHED CUSTOM OR CONSENT, (BUT ASK FOR ADVICE IF YOU'RE UNSURE)

Many areas of open country like moorland, fell and coastal areas, especially those of the National Trust and some commons.

Some woods and forests, especially those owned by the Forestry Commission.

Country Parks and picnic sites.

Most beaches.

Canal towpaths.

Some private paths and tracks. Consent sometimes extends to riding horses and pedal cycles.

FOR YOUR INFORMATION

County councils and London boroughs maintain and record rights-of-way, and register commons. Obstruction, dangerous animals, harassment and misleading signs on rights-of-way are illegal and you should report them to the county council.

Paths across fields can be ploughed, but must normally be reinstated within two weeks.

Landowners can require you to leave land to which you have no right of access.

Motor vehicles are normally permitted only on roads, byways and some 'Roads Used as Public Paths'.

Follow any local bye-laws.

AND, WHEREVER YOU GO, FOLLOW THE COUNTRY CODE

Enjoy the countryside and respect its life and work.

Guard against all risk of fire.

Fasten all gates.

Keep your dogs under close control.

Keep to public paths across farmland.

Use gates and stiles to cross fences, hedges and walls.

Leave livestock, crops and machinery alone.

Take your litter home.

Help to keep all water clean.

Protect wildlife, plants and trees.

Take special care on country roads.

Make no unnecessary noise.

This Charter is for practical guidance in England and Wales only. It was prepared by the Countryside Commission.

Addresses of Useful Organizations

British Trust for Conservation Volunteers
36 St Mary's Street
Wallingford
Oxfordshire OX10 0EU
Tel: (0491) 39766

Cornwall Trust for Nature Conservation
Five Acres
Allet
Truro TR4 9DJ
Tel: (0872) 73939

Council for National Parks
45 Shelton Street
London WC2H 9HJ
Tel: (071) 240 3603

Countryside Commission
John Dower House
Crescent Place
Cheltenham
Glos GL50 3RA
Tel: (0242) 521381

Countryside Commission
South West Regional Office
Bridge House
Sion Place
Clifton Down
Bristol BS8 4AS
Tel: (0272) 739966

Dartmoor National Park Authority
Parke
Haytor Road
Bovey Tracey
Devon TQ13 9JQ
Tel: (0626) 832093

Devon Wildlife Trust
188 Sidwell Street
Exeter EX4 6RD
Tel: (0392) 79244

Dorset AONB/Dorset Heritage Coast
Dorset County Planning Dept.
County Hall
Dorchester DT1 1XJ
Tel: (0305) 251000

Dorset Trust for Nature Conservation
39 Christchurch Road
Bournemouth
Dorset BH1 3NS
Tel: (0202) 554241

East Devon Heritage Coast
c/o Devon County Council
County Hall
Topsham Road
Exeter EX2 4QH
Tel: (0392) 382000

English Nature
South West Regional Office
Roughmoor
Bishop's Hull
Taunton
Somerset TA1 5AA
Tel: (0823) 283211

Exmoor National Park Authority
Exmoor House
Dulverton
Somerset TA22 9HL
Tel: (0398) 23665

Isles of Scilly Environmental Trust
Hamewith
The Parade
St Mary's
Isles of Scilly TR21 0LP
Tel: (0720) 22153/22156

Mendip Hills AONB
Charterhouse Centre
Nr Blagdon
Bristol BS18 6XR
Tel: (0761) 62338

National Trust
36 Queen Anne's Gate
London SW1H 9AS
Tel: (071) 222 9251

National Trust Regional Offices:
Cornwall Regional Office
Lanhydrock
Bodmin
Cornwall PL30 4DE
Tel: (0208) 74281

Devon Regional Office
Killerton House
Broadclyst
Exeter
Devon EX5 3LE
Tel: (0392) 881691

Wessex Regional Office
Stourton
Warminster
Wiltshire BA12 6QD
Tel: (0747) 840560

North Cornwall Heritage Coast
c/o North Cornwall District Council
3 and 5 Barn Lane
Bodmin
Cornwall PL31 1LZ
Tel: (0208) 74121

Ordnance Survey
Romsey Road
Maybush
Southampton SO9 4DH
Tel: (0703) 792764

Quantock Hills AONB Information Centre
Castle Street
Nether Stowey
Bridgwater
Somerset TA15 1LM

Ramblers' Association
1–5 Wandsworth Road
London SW8 2XX
Tel: (071) 582 6878

South Cornwall Heritage Coast
c/o Borough Council Offices
39 Penwinnick Road
St Austell
Cornwall PL25 5DR

South West Water Plc
Peninsula House
Rydon Lane
Exeter EX2 7HR
Tel (0392) 219666

West Country Tourist Board
Trinity Court
37 Southernhay East
Exeter EX1 1QS
Tel: (0392) 76351

INDEX

Page numbers in italics refer to illustrations.